EDUCATION IN DEPRIVED AREAS

PERSPECTIVES ON EDUCATION POLICY

1   *The National Curriculum Beyond 2000: The QCA and the aims of education*
    Richard Aldrich and John White

2   *The Post-Dearing Agenda for Quality and Standards in Higher Education*
    Roger Brown

3   *Do Howard Gardner's Multiple Intelligences Add Up?*
    John White

4   *Information and Communication Technology and Education*
    David Guile

5   *Review of Recent Research on the Achievement of Girls in Single-Sex Schools*
    Jannette Elwood and Caroline Gipps

6   *Can Effective Schools be Inclusive Schools?*
    Ingrid Lunt and Brahm Norwich

7   *The Grammar School Question: A review of research on comprehensive
    and selective education*
    David Crook, Sally Power, Geoff Whitty

8   *The Use of Value Added Information in Judging School Performance*
    Harvey Goldstein, Pan Huiqi, Terry Rath and Nigel Hill

9   *Can School Improvement Overcome the Effects of Disadvantage? Revised edition*
    Peter Mortimore and Geoff Whitty

10 *The Effectiveness of Early Interventions*
    Christine Oliver and Marjorie Smith

11 *Communication Skills and the Knowledge Economy: Language, literacy and the
    production of meaning*
    Fiona Doloughan

12 *Education in Deprived Areas: Outcomes, inputs and processes*
    Sally Power, Simon Warren, David Gillborn, Alison Clark,
    Sally Thomas and Kelly Coate

Institute of Education
University of London

Education in Deprived
Areas: Outcomes, inputs
and processes

SALLY POWER
SIMON WARREN
DAVID GILLBORN
ALISON CLARK
SALLY THOMAS
KELLY COATE

© Institute of Education 2002

Institute of Education University of London
20 Bedford Way
London WC1H 0AL

Pursuing Excellence in Education

British Library Cataloguing in Publication Data:
A catalogue record for this publication is
available from the British Library

ISBN 0-85473-642-5

Produced in Great Britain by
RICOH Document Services
Institute of Education University of London

CONTENTS

Acknowledgements   vi

Foreword   vii

1   Introduction   1

2   The geography of attainment   8

3   Financial and 'real' inputs   28

4   Outputs and processes   50

5   Conclusion and discussion   64

References   67

Appendices   78

ACKNOWLEDGEMENTS

We would like to thank the following people for their help in providing information in connection with the review:

Christine Agambar and David Read, Ofsted
Tony Martin, Trevor Knight and Audrey Brown, Analytical Services, DfES
Vanessa Scarborough, Social Exclusion Unit
Dr George Smith, University of Oxford
Dr Stephen Gorard, University of Cardiff
Alex Gibson, Portsmouth University
Ian McCallum, Freelance Education Research Consultant
Dr Louis Murray, University of Portsmouth

We would also like to thank the following colleagues at the Institute of Education, University of London for their help:

Professor Peter Mortimore
Professor Geoff Whitty
Solange Davin
Ian Plewis
Ken Spours
Professor Ros Levačić
Peter Earley

Finally, thanks to Cate Knowles, Administrator, Education Policy Research Unit, and Julie Thomas for helping compile the report.

All omissions and errors in the report remain our responsibility.

Foreword

In September 1998, the Social Exclusion Unit (SEU) published the report *Bringing Britain Together*.[1] This paints a picture of a divided country with deprived neighbourhoods experiencing a range of interlocking problems, such as high levels of unemployment, crime, ill health and poor education and housing. It also shows how the gap between deprived neighbourhoods and the rest of the country has widened over the last 20 years and analyses why previous initiatives to deal with these problems have failed. It argues that a major national effort is going to be needed if these areas are to improve.

Following the publication of this report, the SEU was tasked by the Prime Minister with drawing up a national strategy for neighbourhood renewal. This strategy – *A New Commitment to Neighbourhood Renewal* – was published in January 2001.[2] It describes new policies, funding and targets, new means of better coordinating local services and empowering communities and new support at regional and national levels for neighbourhood renewal. All these measures are aimed at narrowing the gap between the most deprived neighbourhoods and the rest of the country in terms of employment, crime, health, skills and housing and the physical environment, through improving these characteristics in absolute terms in deprived areas. The vision the strategy will contribute towards is that within 10–20 years, no one should be seriously disadvantaged by where they live.

In drawing up this strategy, it became clear that mainstream public services (like health, education and law and order) need to be the Government's main instruments and need to be equipped for this job. Given their national coverage and the scale of resources available to them, they need to work towards addressing the problems of deprived neighbourhoods if they are to be dealt with effectively and sustainably.

Despite repeated calls over the years for mainstream public sector programmes to be 'bent' towards addressing the needs of poor areas, there is little evidence that this has happened enough. Rather, there is much anecdotal evidence that, for a range of reasons – some more obvious than others – the performance of mainstream public services has often differed between deprived and non-deprived areas. It has been argued that they perform less well – in terms of the quality of their outputs and outcomes – in deprived areas. But when the SEU was drawing the national strategy on neighbourhood renewal together, hard evidence to back up these arguments was scarce and had not been analysed as a whole. Studies had been done on differences in terms of inputs like expenditure[3], but those on outputs and outcomes were more scarce or focused on narrow aspects of a service.

The SEU therefore commissioned three literature reviews to draw together what evidence existed in order to inform the development of the national strategy for neighbourhood renewal. For education, health and law enforcement forces we asked that the relevant literature be reviewed in order to identify what – if any – hard evidence exists about the performance of each of these mainstream public services in deprived areas compared to that in non-deprived areas.

This report is the outcome of the review of the literature on education services. The authors were asked to assess the relevant literature (going back 10–15 years) and data and to analyse:

- what hard evidence there is of differential or equivalent levels of quality (outputs) and performance (outcomes) in education services in deprived as compared with non-deprived areas
- if there are differences, what the nature of those differences are
- whether there are differences in people's access to these services in deprived and non-deprived areas
- how effective or otherwise mainstream education services are in the most deprived neighbourhoods as compared to non-deprived neighbourhoods

- whether effectiveness and access differ in deprived areas for different social groups (e.g. black and ethnic minority people, young people, elderly people, disabled people)
- what the available evidence suggests in terms of understanding the causes of any differences in delivery and performance (for example, to what degree any different outcomes are supply or demand driven; to what degree they are related to differences in funding, recruitment and retention, etc) and the implications for public policy
- what the evidence tells us about the resource problems faced by public services in deprived areas even when there is no clear link to performance.[4]

The available evidence on performance demonstrates that – as expected – outcomes in schools serving deprived populations are poorer than those serving non-deprived populations. It paints a complex picture of the possible reasons and causes for these differences – which are probably multiple and interact with each other – but the differences remain clear.

The main response to this evidence, alongside similar evidence from other sources, has been to incorporate in the National Strategy for Neighbourhood Renewal two 'floor' targets for educational attainment and additional funding in order to meet them. Thus the DfES now has targets to ensure that by 2004 no school has fewer than 25 per cent of pupils getting five or more A*–C grade GCSE passes, and that no Local Education Authority has fewer than 38 per cent of pupils achieving these results. The 2001–2004 spending review allocated an additional £11 billion to education and training, which will help achieve these targets.

The types of measure that will be deployed in this include extending the Excellence in Cities programme to cover more areas and schools, allocating funding from the School Improvement Grant to around 500 schools to improve performance, and giving special help to the most seriously under-achieving schools, including twinning with other schools, using head teachers as consultants, expanding the National Mentoring Project, and considering a Fresh Start for every school where fewer than 15 per cent of pupils get five good GCSE passes in three consecutive years. In addition, at least £600 million has been allocated over the next three years to help tackle truancy and school exclusions and help schools manage difficult behaviour more effectively. The evidence now indicates that the combination of targeted extra support to those schools and pupils that face the greatest challenge, as well as universal policies such as the literacy and numeracy strategies, are making a difference. The tests and examinations in 2000 and the Youth Cohort Study indicate that at last achievement differences are beginning to narrow. Building on this early progress is a key priority. Similar measures to improve health, employment and housing and to reduce crime in deprived areas are also part of the National Strategy for Neighbourhood Renewal.

The Social Exclusion Unit found it valuable to have the evidence reviewed in this report brought together in one place. Inevitably, further work on these issues has been undertaken since the drafting of this report was completed; however, we hope that, nonetheless, others find the report useful too.

SOCIAL EXCLUSION UNIT
Cabinet Office

[1] SEU (1998), *Bringing Britain Together: A national strategy for neighbourhood renewal*. London: The Stationery Office.

[2] SEU (2001), *A New Commitment to Neighbourhood Renewal: National Strategy Action Plan*.

[3] See for example, Bramley, G. *et al.* (1998), *Where Does Public Spending Go?: Pilot Study To Analyse the Flows of Public Expenditure into Local Areas*. London: DETR.

[4] We did not ask the authors to assess current policies and their actual or potential impact on performance. Indeed, in many cases, the literature and data reviewed inevitably predated current policies.

1
Introduction

Recent research (e.g. Hills, 1996; ONS, 2000) into the distribution of wealth and income has pointed to increasing social polarisation in the United Kingdom. In the post-war period up to the late 1970s there was a relative reduction in economic inequalities. Since 1979, however, this trend has been reversed. For instance, the living standards of people in the bottom two- or three-tenths of the income distribution have not significantly risen since 1979. This contrasts dramatically with those at the top of the distribution, whose standard of living has risen faster than the average.

The evidence paints a picture of rising overall standards of living occurring alongside an increasing social polarisation of society. Parallel to this greater social polarisation is the increase in the geographical concentration of poverty (Green, 1996). Poverty tends to be more concentrated in the North than the South; in large cities, particularly inner London, than rural areas; and in areas supported by a narrow industrial base (e.g. mining, heavy manufacturing and coastal industries). Inner London and Merseyside are particularly affected by severe social and economic problems (DETR, 1998; 2000).

Within this geography of poverty there is a particular patterning by ethnic group. While ethnic minorities are disproportionately located in deprived inner-city areas, there are significant differences between groups. Some minorities, specifically those of Chinese and Indian heritage, 'enjoy incomes very similar to those of the white population': in contrast, those of Bangladeshi and Pakistani heritage are 'four times as likely to be in poverty as white people' (Berthoud, 1998:46). The picture for people of 'African' ethnic heritage is still relatively unclear, but those self-identifying as 'Black Caribbean' and 'Black Other' are twice as likely to be unemployed as their white counterparts (Berthoud, 1998; Modood *et al.*, 1997). The situation is especially severe for young men of Caribbean heritage (Berthoud, 1999). It is important to recognise that under certain conditions the ethnic dimension of 'disadvantage' can be related to factors independent of place of residence. A clear example is experience of racist victimisation. Similarly, it has been argued that: 'Levels of income are less influenced by where people from minority ethnic groups live now, but more so by factors such as who they are and where they came from' (Chahal, 2000).

Notwithstanding the qualifications noted above, available evidence shows that people who live in severely disadvantaged areas are proportionately more likely to have poor educational outcomes. There have been several attempts to break this connection. Of particular relevance here is the 1967 Plowden Report (Plowden Committee, 1967) which recommended that extra assistance be given to schools with disadvantaged intakes. This in turn led to the establishment of Educational Priority Areas (EPAs) – localities and schools that were identified as being deprived through a variety of indicators.

By the mid-1980s, however, EPAs had all but disappeared (Smith, 1987) and the focus for promoting educational achievement shifted away from the *external* circumstances experienced by schools and towards their *internal* attributes, in particular towards how schools were to be managed and made more accountable. The devolution of school budgets together with open enrolment and the publication of pupil attainment data were intended to provide the necessary impetus to drive up educational attainment in *all* schools.

The outcome of these policies is still being debated, but even if their effects are less damaging than some reviews of the evidence suggest, broader economic polarisation and greater geographical concentration of poverty need addressing. Indeed, the Social Exclusion Unit itself, its strategy for neighbourhood renewal (SEU, 1998a) and the work of the Policy Action Teams are responses to this growing social divide. There is now a clear need for 'positive discrimination and the effective targeting of human and material resources' (Mortimore and Whitty, 1999:168). This need is reflected in the reappearance of area-based initiatives, such as Education Action Zones and Excellence in Cities, and a growing recognition of the complex relations between locality, service and social exclusion (Mortimore and Mortimore, 1999; Sparkes, 1999). In order to maximise the potential of future neighbourhood strategies, a review of the quality, performance and impact of education services is therefore both timely and important.

THE OBJECTIVES OF THE REVIEW

The objective of this research is to review the available literature and data in order to identify what – if any – hard evidence exists about the performance of mainstream public sector education services in deprived areas compared to non-deprived areas. More specifically, the review has attempted to provide an analysis of the following research questions:

1. What evidence is there of differential or equivalent levels of quality (outputs) and performance (outcomes) in education services in deprived as compared to non-deprived areas?
2. What is the nature of those differences?
3. What are the differences in people's access to services?
4. How effective are education services?
5. Do effectiveness and access differ in deprived areas for different social groups?
6. What are the causes of differences in delivery and performance, and the implications for public policy?
7. What are the resource problems faced by public services, even when there is no clear link to performance?

THE STRUCTURE OF THE REVIEW

The research questions outlined above are complex and overlapping. In order to analyse the data in a systematic way, we have structured the evidence into the kind of input-outcome model that is often employed in cost-effectiveness analyses and school effectiveness research:

$$Inputs \quad \rightarrow \quad Processes \quad \rightarrow \quad Outputs \quad \rightarrow \quad Outcomes$$

Clearly, its purpose here is somewhat different, as we are using it as an organising device through which differences in identified outcomes can be explored in terms of variations in the input and/or variations in the quality (output) of institutional process. The relationship between the model, its elements and the research questions (RQs) listed above is outlined in Table 1.1 below.

TABLE 1.1: RELATIONSHIP BETWEEN THE INPUT-OUTCOME MODEL, ITS ELEMENTS AND THE RESEARCH QUESTIONS

Financial inputs ⇓	LEA Government programmes (e.g. EiC, EAZs) Private sponsorship
⇑ Real resource inputs ⇓	Pupils Capacity Access Personnel (teachers) Volunteers (governors)
Processes (outputs) ⇓	School effectiveness School ethos Curriculum coverage Home-school liaison Special provision
Intermediate outcomes ⇓	Student participation Exclusions Student dropout
Outcomes ⇓	Examination attainments Affective outcomes Continuation to next stage of education

Source: Adapted from Scheerens, 1990 and Levačić, 2000

There are difficulties with the framework inasmuch as it is not always easy to compartmentalise aspects of the education process into only one of the categories. Parental involvement, for instance, could be represented as an 'input', an 'output' or an intermediate 'outcome'. In addition, neighbourhood socio-economic attributes become embodied as 'pupil input' – an approach for which school effectiveness research has been criticised (Angus, 1993). However, despite the difficulties, we believe that the model provides an analytical framework that can facilitate assessing the relevant factors which 'make a difference' and which might help identify the more appropriate policy responses.

Chapter 2 of the review begins by looking at evidence of outcomes in order to establish the extent to which there is a 'geography of attainment'. Chapter 3 examines evidence of a relationship between deprived areas, educational outcomes and inputs. Chapter 4 explores evidence concerning the relationship between the processes of institutional quality (outputs) and outcomes. Finally, Chapter 5 concludes with a brief discussion of some of the implications. The appendices contain information about datasets that can be used to illuminate further these issues.

RESEARCH METHODS

In order to undertake the review, electronic databases and library catalogues were searched using a variety of descriptors in order to try and capture as many sources of published data as possible (see Appendix 1). To ensure greatest relevance, we only looked at research reported in the last ten years which focused primarily on the English situation. Each of the studies was then analysed using a proforma (see Appendix 2) to ascertain as far as possible:

- the study aims and objective
- methods and robustness of data collection and analysis
- the extent to which comparisons between deprived and non-deprived areas can be deduced and/or inferred
- the identity and purpose of the funders and the extent to which this may have influenced the selection and presentation of data
- reported implications for policy and practice
- relevance to the national strategy of neighbourhood renewal.

Establishing relevance to the review was complicated because of difficulties in defining the key terms 'education service' and 'deprived' and 'non-deprived' areas. We took an early decision to omit pre-school provision from the review because it is such a mixed economy that looking at public sector services alone would misrepresent the situation. We also excluded higher education services, because the linkage with area is more distant. Material relating to post-16 provision was included where we considered it had a bearing on mapping out differential outcomes, but the quality and broader outputs were not looked at.

It is the issue of the 'area' focus that caused most difficulties. Data collected at regional or LEA level are often too broad and fail to capture the 'neighbourhood' dimension that the review needed. Other data tend to be collected at institutional level. These data certainly give an indication of the levels of individual disadvantage within one school, but its location within a deprived area then has to be inferred. There are problems with relating the attributes of a neighbourhood to the socio-economic profile of a school. Some schools, particularly where they are selective, may not draw pupils from their local neighbourhood. Postcode analyses of pupils (e.g. Gibson and Asthana, 1999) have problems, but do attempt to examine this issue.

We anticipated these difficulties and realised that the definitions of 'area' and 'neighbourhood', and how these related to levels of deprivation, would always be fairly loose. Data of 'best fit' for the purposes of the review were identified – which meant that on occasions neighbourhood deprivation was inferred from geographical location, assessments of housing quality or proportions of pupils eligible for free school meals (FSM). In many cases the data relate to schools *serving* deprived populations rather than schools *located* in deprived neighbourhoods. If nothing else we hope that this review highlights the need for more systematic research to be undertaken which considers neighbourhood factors in addition to pupil- and school-level attributes.

2
The geography of attainment

In order to consider whether there is a geography of attainment, we need to consider how issues of local deprivation and educational performance are operationalised in the research.

Studies relating local deprivation to school outcomes are usually based on the socio-economic attributes of the pupil population – in particular, the proportion of students eligible for free school meals (FSM) or other socio-economic attributes associated with pupil postcodes. It needs to be remembered, however, that some schools, particularly secondary schools, serve catchment areas that extend beyond their local neighbourhood, and that this measure does not therefore necessarily reflect the attributes of the school's locality. The boundaries of Local Education Authorities (LEAs) provide another dimension of 'locality' that can be related to indicators of educational performance and social deprivation, but LEAs can cover quite extensive areas and usually contain many different types of neighbourhood. A few studies that we have consulted do try to link educational outcomes to neighbourhood in a variety of different ways, but these remain relatively rare.

The conventional measure of educational outcome is attainment in standardised assessment tasks at Key Stages and especially in GCSEs. In addition to research on these outcomes, we have also looked at the available evidence on other outcomes, such as progression to the next stage of education. Research on broader outcomes, such as subsequent income and area crime statistics, cannot be considered here, but are also likely to be vital to the overall process of neighbourhood renewal.

As well as 'end-point' outcomes, this chapter also considers studies that have looked at more intermediate outcomes. Of particular significance here are studies that focus on levels of student participation, as measured through attendance rates and exclusion.

Currently, relatively little work has evaluated the relationship between locality and the affective outcomes in education. Thomas and Smees' analysis of academic and attitudinal outcomes in Scotland (1998; 2000) suggests that the differences between schools in terms of changing pupils' attitudes are small in comparison with the results for academic outcomes.

THE GEOGRAPHY OF EDUCATIONAL OUTCOMES

Overall, school outcomes in deprived areas are worse than those in non-deprived areas, whether these are measured in terms of qualifications, attendance or exclusions. Levels of academic attainment have risen across the country, but they have not risen evenly. Smith *et al.* (1997:135) found that GCSE results improved less in schools in deprived areas than in non-deprived areas. In the most disadvantaged LEAs (the 25 per cent with the highest proportion of families in lower socio-economic groups) just under 20 per cent gained 5+ grades A–C in 1988, rising to about 32 per cent in 1996. For the most advantaged areas (the 25 per cent with the highest proportion of non-manual families) the change was from just under 30 per cent to 48 per cent. Evidence for this trend is supported in the Policy Action Team's *School Plus* report (DfEE, 2000a).

Recent figures published by the DfEE (DfEE, 2000b) suggest that the gap may be starting to narrow. Pupils in inner-city schools have shown improvements in English and maths at Key Stage 2. Tower Hamlets in East London was the most improved LEA, with the highest percentage increase in the number of children achieving KS2 (Level 4) in both English and maths. For example, maths scores in the borough rose from 45 per cent achieving Level 4 and above in 1998 to 68 per cent in 2000, a 23 per cent increase compared to a national average increase of 3 per cent. Even so, the gap remains wide – both at LEA, institutional and neighbourhood level.

LEA-level patterns

Across LEAs, the mean percentage of pupils in a maintained secondary school attaining 5 A*–C GCSE grades in 1999 was 46 per cent (Ofsted, 2000c). However, there is considerable variation across LEAs – with the mean percentage ranging from 61.1 per cent to 23.4 per cent. This variation also exists in results at KS2. The lowest performing LEAs are also among the most deprived areas in the country as recorded in the latest indicators of deprivation (DETR, 2000).

TABLE 2.1: LEAS WITH LOWEST PERCENTAGE ACHIEVING LEVEL 4 AND ABOVE IN KEY
STAGE 2 ENGLISH IN THE YEAR 2000[1]

LEA	% achieving Level 4 and above in KS2 English
Nottingham	60%
Hackney	61%
Haringey	63%
Greenwich	63%
Leicester	64%
Newham	64%

Source: DfEE, 2000b

School-level patterns

The relationship between level of deprivation and outcome is clearly
evident at institutional level. An analysis (Beckett, 2000) of recent DfEE
data graphically illustrates the relationship between GCSE
performance in non-selective schools and the number of pupils within
a school being eligible for FSM.

In contrast to 44 per cent of pupils achieving 5 or more GCSEs at A*–C
in the median mainstream school in England, the percentage for the
median non-selective school with high levels of disadvantage (defined
here as schools with between 35–50 per cent of pupils eligible for FSM)
was only 24 per cent. Similarly, at KS2, while 69 per cent of pupils
nationally reached Level 4 in English, in disadvantaged schools this was
54 per cent (DfEE, 2000a).

The achievement of pupils in schools with very high concentrations
of economically disadvantaged pupils (more than 50 per cent FSM
pupils) is considerably lower than pupils' achievement in other schools.
As Table 2.2 shows, the students in these schools achieve far fewer
GCSEs at the higher grades than the national average (Thomas, 2000).

FIGURE 2.1: FSM ELIGIBILITY AND % OF PUPILS IN MEDIAN SCHOOL GAINING 5+ GCSEs AT A*–C IN NON-SELECTIVE SCHOOLS

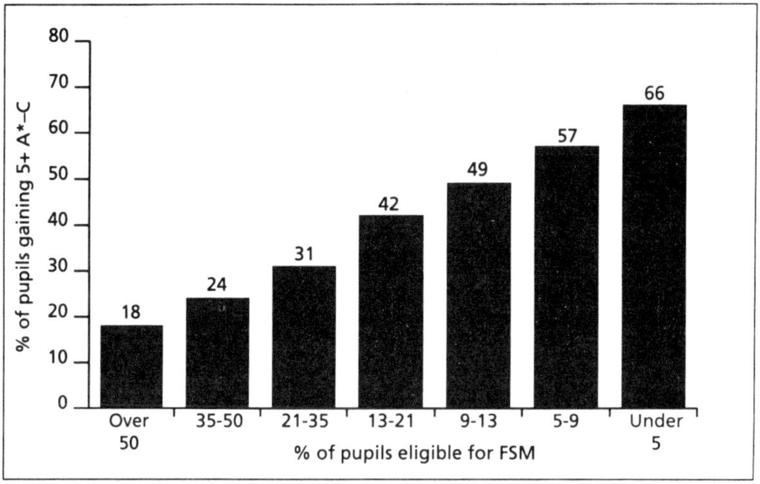

Source: Adapted from Beckett, 2000 and Ofsted, 2000c

TABLE 2.2: GCSE ATTAINMENTS IN ALL MAINTAINED SCHOOLS AND THOSE WITH MORE THAN 50 PER CENT OF PUPILS ELIGIBLE FOR FSM

	All maintained schools	Schools > 50% FSM
Median GCSE/GNVQ score	37.1 points†	24.3 points††
Median % pupils 5+ A*–C	44%	18%

† Equivalent to 5 grade Cs and 2 grade Bs
†† Equivalent to 4 grade Cs and 1 grade D
Source: Thomas, 2000

Although there is a clear correlation between pupil deprivation (as measured by FSM eligibility) and school performance, schools with apparently similar intakes can have widely differing achievements. As *Excellence in Schools* (DfEE, 1997) reports, some schools with less than 5 per cent of their pupils receiving FSM had lower KS2 English results than other with over 40 per cent receiving FSM.

The relationship between deprivation and attainment has also been explored using pupil postcode data. Where these data are systematically collected it is possible to assign to pupils, and therefore schools, socio-economic information derived from the Census. McCallum and Redhead (2000) use this method to examine the correlations between social factors and GCSE performance. Their analysis shows that all significant socio-economic factors (e.g. parental occupation and education, home ownership) are correlated with GCSE performance. A similar study of KS2 data from almost 5,000 pupils at schools in Ealing (McCallum and Redhead, 1998) shows that pupils from homes located in the 'most favourable areas' (as indicated by percentages from the highest social categories) score more highly than others in every subject. They comment that the relationship between reading score group and the percentage eligible for FSM is 'particularly striking'.

These studies provide a better understanding of the relationship between local deprivation and school performance. However, it needs to be remembered that the local area attributes inferred from the postcodes are based on the 1991 Census data which are now dated.

'Neighbourhood'-level patterns

The above comparisons are based on data gathered at LEA level or at school level, which do not capture local neighbourhood differences.

A few studies have looked at attainment in a locality, using a variety of indicators of disadvantage. Smith (1999), for instance, uses the DETR Index of Local Deprivation and 1994 DfEE data to show that pupils who achieved no GCSE graded results are highly concentrated in a small number of schools. One-fifth were concentrated in 203 schools in England – only 6 per cent of all maintained secondary schools. Smith notes that 58 per cent of these schools were located within two miles of one of the 320 large deprived social housing estates.

Benn and Chitty (1996) conducted a detailed questionnaire survey of comprehensive schools in Britain and collected data on a range of neighbourhood variables. Schools were asked about the location and intake of their school in terms of the 'type' of locality (large city [200,000+], town [5,000–20,000], suburban area, village [under 5,000] or countryside), the kind of housing pupils 'mainly' came from (council or housing association, private residential, mix of council and private, substandard, mix of council, private and substandard) and the social attributes of pupils (ethnicity, EAL, social class background, FSM and turnover rates).

The problem with this particular survey is that the response rate was relatively low (around 37 per cent), so that its findings cover only a minority of secondary schools. There are likely to be significant differences in the attributes of responding and non-responding schools (Power, 1997). In addition, schools make their own assessment of locality and housing attributes. While it could be argued that schools know their neighbourhoods and can provide an accurate assessment, there may well be variations in response. There may be a tendency, for instance, for some schools to over-represent the levels of disadvantage that they face. Despite these limits, Benn and Chitty's survey clearly confirms the finding from the other studies that schools in deprived areas do not perform as well as those in non-deprived areas.

Urban, rural and coastal resort deprivation

Benn and Chitty's (1996) survey also shows that schools in city areas perform particularly poorly. Indeed, it often seems as if the term 'inner city' has become synonymous with deprivation, ignoring the extent to which inner cities may also contain pockets of extreme affluence. We were therefore interested in ascertaining whether any research has looked into the educational performance of different *types* of deprived areas. For instance, are outcomes in deprived rural areas different from outcomes in deprived inner-city areas? It had also been put to us that there might be a 'coastal rim' effect in Britain.

Research supports the commonly held assumption that it is inner-city schools whose performance is weakest. As *Excellence in Cities* (DfEE, 1999a) outlines, only 33 per cent of inner-city pupils get five or more GCSE grades A*–C. This puts them well behind the national average of 46 per cent and behind schools in other London and metropolitan authorities, whose own performance is weaker than that of schools in unitary and shire authorities.

We could find no research findings relating schools in 'poor' rural or coastal areas to lower attainment levels. It is possible that rural or coastal deprivation is insufficiently concentrated to be reflected at the available levels of analysis. For instance, a 'coastal rim' effect may be identifiable in individual institutions but not show up in measures of LEA outcomes. Rural deprivation does not tend to show up, even at institutional level. Benn and Chitty's survey (1996:191) reports that schools in villages had higher percentages in the top 20 per cent attainment range (21.5 per cent) compared with schools in the cities (13.6 per cent). Schools in the countryside and villages averaged 47.5 per cent of pupils with five GCSE A*–C grades, well above the survey average of 39.3 per cent.

Housing type

Through using more sensitive definitions of neighbourhood, Benn and Chitty's (1996) survey does reveal some variations in area-based outcomes. Housing quality, for instance, is likely to provide a better indicator of local deprivation than locality descriptions (such as 'city', 'suburban', 'rural'). Their data reveal that almost nine out of ten (89 per cent) comprehensive schools drawing from substandard housing and nearly two-thirds (63 per cent) drawing from council housing had 31 per cent or more of their pupils entitled to FSM. This is compared with only 1.3 per cent of comprehensive schools drawing from private residential or owner-occupied housing areas in 1994.

Comparison of outcomes by predominant housing type served reveal stark polarisation of performance. Over a quarter (26.4 per cent) of schools in the top 20 per cent of attainment draw from pupils in private housing, whereas less than one in ten (9.8 per cent) of those drawing from substandard housing and 8.6 per cent of those drawing from council housing are in the top 20 per cent of attaining schools. Similar patterns are evident in relation to GCSEs and A levels (Table 2.3).

TABLE 2.3: SCHOOL LEVEL ATTAINMENTS BY PREDOMINANT TYPE OF HOUSING SERVED

	GCSE A–C pass rate	A level grade point average
Substandard housing	18.2%	8.0
Council housing	23.2%	9.2
Mixed (council and private)	42.2%	13.4
Private housing	52.1%	14.2

Source: Benn and Chitty, 1996

PROGRESSION TO THE NEXT STAGE

Just as educational attainments have risen overall, the proportion of 16–18 year olds in full-time education has increased in the last decade to 70 per cent in 1998 (SEU, 1999). However, during the same period,

26 per cent of the age group were receiving no education or training and around 7 per cent were not in any education, training or employment.

There are strong regional trends in participation. Staying-on rates in full-time education are higher in London, the South East and South West than in other regions, particularly those in the North of England (SEU, 1999). While the high London rate reveals the inadequacy of using metropolitan location as a proxy for disadvantage, it needs to be noted that inner London has a much higher rate of non-participation than outer London. There is a strong correlation between the most deprived local authority districts and non-participation rates in further education and training (SEU, 1999).

The North-South divide in staying on beyond compulsory schooling is widely recorded. Payne (1995; 1998) found a widening gap between the staying-on rate of 16 and 17 year olds in Greater London, which had the highest staying-on rate (80 per cent), and the North, which had the lowest (60 per cent). Regional differences in participation in education and training post-16 is strong even after GCSE performance is taken into account, particularly for lower-achieving young people. For example, in both medium (5+ graded results with 1–4 A*–C grades) and low (less than these grades) results bands, there was a difference of 23 percentage points between staying-on rates in the North and in Greater London (Payne, 1998). In Ainley et al.'s (1999) study of three 'sub-regions' (up to 750,000 people), a smaller analysis at ward level reveals that all those wards known informally to be of working-class housing or social deprivation areas (such as those in South East London) had staying-on rates post-16 well below 30 per cent.

An analysis (Cheng, 1995) of Cohort 5 from the Youth Cohort Study also highlights neighbourhood patterns. It is unusual for a YCS study because it combines YCS data with data from the Schools Census and the Database of Teacher Records, LEA information on education provision, the 1991 census and the local labour market data. In particular, the study was designed to analyse the influence of school type on staying-on rates in education. This analysis backs up other studies by finding that GCSE grades are the most important predictor of staying on. However, Cheng also found that staying-on rates were lower in schools with high rates of teacher turnover and high proportions of FSM students – all attributes associated with schools located in deprived areas. Cheng used one measure, the percentage of lone parents in the ward, as a single proxy for adverse social and economic conditions. Pupils were less likely to stay on in areas with high proportions of lone-parent families than in areas with low proportions of lone-parent families, even when students from similar backgrounds are compared. Based on this finding, Cheng suggests that the economic and cultural deprivation of inner-city neighbourhoods may have negative effects on staying-on rates. Not surprisingly, the relationship between deprivation, neighbourhood type and pro-gression endures into higher education (HEFCE, 1997).

OUTCOMES FOR DIFFERENT SOCIAL GROUPS

Issues also arise in relation to how education services are variously experienced by different social groups. The evidence shows that there is no simple relationship between area and 'racial'/ethnic composition. As levels of deprivation and demographic concentrations vary between ethnic groups, it is not possible to consider area effects separately or to identify adequate samples of students from certain minority groups in non-deprived areas at the current time. Nevertheless, minority ethnic students are proportionately more likely to be living in deprived areas.

Thus, Benn and Chitty's (1996) survey reports that those schools with minority ethnic groups also had a higher working-class intake: 81 per cent of schools with African Caribbean groups, 71 per cent of schools with Indian, 76 per cent with Chinese and 72 per cent with Irish concentrations also had high intakes of working-class students. They also had higher proportions eligible for FSM.

While it is true that ethnic minorities tend to be geographically concentrated in inner-city areas, they are not necessarily concentrated in disadvantaged areas. There is evidence to suggest that certain minority ethnic groups, particularly African Caribbean communities, are becoming less geographically concentrated (Peach, 1996). We raise this issue because it is important not to collapse different processes of disadvantage (social class, 'race', gender) into one index. The effect of these different processes would need to be disaggregated before an area effect could be positively defined. For example, compared with their white counterparts, young people from each of the principal minority ethnic groups are more likely to remain in full-time education post-16. This is despite the relatively lower average attainments of some groups, notably African Caribbean, Pakistani and Bangladeshi young people (Drew, 1995; Modood and Shiner, 1994; Pathak, 2000). The reasons for the greater participation of minority ethnic young people are not certain, but among the most likely explanations are greater motivation and parental support plus strategies to avoid unemployment and to offset the impact of racism in the labour market (Gillborn and Gipps, 1996). Drew *et al.* (1992) show that 70 per cent of Asian students and 66 per cent of African Caribbean students reported family support for staying on, compared with 48 per cent of white students. Nevertheless, the patterns of differential educational attainment and inequalities of opportunity by ethnicity are visible in the rather different routes which minority young people follow. South Asian students, for example, tend to follow traditional 'academic' courses, while African Caribbean young people are more likely to pursue vocational courses (Gillborn and Gipps, 1996).

A similar pattern of differential experiences and attainment can be identified in relation to minority ethnic students in secondary schools. Although the overall level of educational attainment rose during the 1990s, an 'attainment gap' exists for certain groups, particularly African Caribbean, Pakistani, Bangladeshi and working-class students more generally. A reanalysis of data on GCSE attainments, produced by the Youth Cohort Study in the late 1980s and 1990s, indicates that the gaps are growing between middle-class and working-class students, and that white attainments overall are significantly outpacing those of African Caribbean students (Demack et al., 2000).[2] Although African Caribbean attainments have risen overall, white students have drawn considerably greater benefit from the changes in attainment at GCSE. The result is that between the mid-1980s and mid-1990s, the so-called 'black/white' gap grew by half as much again (Gillborn and Youdell, 2000).

Within each ethnic group, pupils from non-manual backgrounds are more likely to achieve five higher-grade passes. However, even after controlling for social class, many inequalities persist. For example, only white pupils improved year on year in both manual and non-manual backgrounds. For most of the period in question, black pupils were less likely to attain five higher-grade passes than their peers of the same social class in any other ethnic group (Gillborn and Mirza, 2000).

The new Ethnic Minority and Traveller Achievement Grant (EMTAG) offers a uniquely detailed glimpse of minority attainment in different LEAs. A hundred and eighteen of the first submissions for EMTAG support, in 1999, have been analysed as part of an independent enquiry (funded by Ofsted) into current levels of performance by 'race', class and gender (Gillborn and Mirza, 2000). This reanalysis shows that there is a considerable variety of performance between different localities. For example, for each of the principal minority ethnic groups, the data reveal at least one LEA where that group is the most likely to achieve at least five higher-grade GCSEs. This finding must be qualified by noting that in some LEAs the proportions are based on small population sizes and that many LEAs gave incomplete returns. Nevertheless, the finding confirms the pattern identified in the late 1990s, in an earlier Ofsted-funded review, that there could be significant differences in minority attainment in some locales (Gillborn and Gipps, 1996). Unfortunately, the EMTAG data are not sufficiently detailed to allow a sound comparison between specific deprived and non-deprived areas. Additionally, although the 1999 EMTAG data highlight LEAs where the national patterns of attainment[3] are apparently contradicted, it is nevertheless true that wider patterns of attainment by ethnicity seem to persist in many areas, especially concerning the lower average achievements of African Caribbean, Bangladeshi and Pakistani young people.

The London Borough of Tower Hamlets received considerable attention in the mid-1990s when it emerged that young people of Bangladeshi ethnic origin, despite the widespread poverty of the area, were now achieving higher average GCSE results than their white counterparts (see Gillborn and Gipps, 1996). This is an important trend, which demonstrates that there is no automatic association between poverty and attainment. Nevertheless, it should be appreciated that average attainments in the borough remain lower than the national average.

A further issue of significance for LEAs such as Tower Hamlets is the relatively high concentration of pupils for whom English is an additional language (EAL). In 1996/97 around 7.5 per cent of all pupils of compulsory school age in England were known to have EAL. These pupils are not evenly distributed across the country; indeed, schools in

London serve almost half of all pupils nationally with EAL (DfEE, 1999d). Several LEAs outside the capital also cater to relatively large proportions of pupils with EAL, notably Birmingham, Bradford, Leicester City and Luton, where a quarter or more of pupils have EAL. It would be very instructive to identify whether EAL pupils (of similar social class and ethnic background) make better progress in some schools or locales, particularly those with higher or lower levels of deprivation. Unfortunately, there is no single database that allows sufficiently detailed analysis to answer that question at present.

It is important to note, however, that EAL is not the uniformly negative barrier to attainment that was once assumed. Indeed, it is clear that once EAL pupils attain a reasonable degree of fluency, they can often outperform their monolingual peers (Gillborn and Mirza, 2000). Some indication of this can be seen from data on the relative performance of schools with different concentrations of EAL pupils. Comparing schools with broadly similar levels of social disadvantage (as indicated by the percentage of pupils known to be eligible for FSM) at KS1, on average, the DfEE reports that 'the performance of schools with the highest intensities of pupils with EAL was generally somewhat below that of all other [similar] schools' (DfEE, 1999d:2). These differences were 'nominal' at KS2 and the situation was reversed by KS4:

> At GCSE the performance of schools with high intensities of pupils with EAL was overall higher than the performance of other schools with equivalent levels of ... disadvantage. (DfEE, 1999d:2)

The current picture of attainment by minority ethnic youth in different locales, therefore, is still somewhat limited. Samples of LEA-level data suggest significant variation in attainment for the same ethnic group but in different parts of the country. Unfortunately, LEA data are not sufficiently detailed to permit the effects of social class, school and locale to be calculated separately. New research, and the introduction of the Common Basic Dataset, may help clarify this picture in the near future, but it is beyond doubt that more attention should focus on this issue.

INTERMEDIATE EDUCATIONAL OUTCOMES
Participation rates

There is wide regional variation in attendance rates. As the Social Exclusion Unit Report (SEU, 1998b) notes, the level of unauthorised absence in Manchester is over four times that in Tyneside and almost nine times that in Oxfordshire. In general, schools serving deprived areas are also likely to have lower rates of participation. The 1995 YCS report (Cheng, 1995) found that the truancy levels in schools serving 'difficult to let' estates was four times the national average. Truancy also appears to be more common in inner-city areas (Casey and Smith, 1995). Benn and Chitty's (1996) survey reports that 50 per cent of schools drawing from mainly working-class homes registered attendance at below 90 per cent compared with only 1 per cent of schools where intakes were predominantly middle class. They argue that where intakes were more mixed, there was dramatic improvement, which they claim provides an example of 'a balanced "mix" producing a leavening effect' (1996:221). As might be expected, metropolitan boroughs had lower attendance rates than the shire counties. That the kind of area is important, rather than just the level of affluence, is evident in the great difference in attendance levels between those schools with intakes mainly from council housing and those drawing from villages and the countryside.

Exclusions

A range of studies has highlighted the very significant rise in exclusions, in both primary and secondary schools, that occurred in the late 1980s and into the late 1990s (Gillborn and Gipps, 1996; SEU, 1998b). The use of exclusions in schools disproportionately affects particular groups of students, with African Caribbean students and those with special educational needs being up to six times more likely to be excluded than their peers. The Social Exclusion Unit's first report, on truancy and exclusion from schools (SEU, 1998b), also notes that children being 'looked after' are ten times more likely to be excluded.

The report sets an ambitious target for a reduction in exclusions of one-third by 2002. There is already evidence of this policy bearing fruit, with a reduction in permanent exclusions being recorded in both 1997/98 and 1998/99. Over these two years, permanent exclusions fell from over 12,000 to around 10,000 (DfEE, 1999c; 2000d). This represents a fall of around 18 per cent of the peak figure (recorded in 1996/97).

Initially there was concern that minority ethnic pupils were not sharing equally in this reduction. When the first overall fall was recorded in 1997/98, for example, there was no fall at all in the rate for Black Caribbean children. More recently, however, minority groups have tended to experience relatively greater reductions. Nevertheless, the over-representation of black children continues in the latest figures. In 1998/99, for example, 0.15 per cent of white children were permanently excluded compared with 0.58 per cent of Black Caribbean, 0.49 per cent of Black Other and 0.21 per cent of Black African children.

The statistical evidence on ethnicity and exclusions is far from perfect. Although ethnic monitoring is being used more widely, national data on the ethnic background of excluded pupils are only available for a four-year period (covering 1995/96, 1996/97, 1997/98 and 1998/99). These limitations notwithstanding, it is possible to identify some broad conclusions. First, of the major ethnic categories for which data are collected, it is only the black groups (defined officially as Black Caribbean, Black African and Black Other) that account for a greater proportion of exclusions than would be expected in view of their representation in the school population. This is true for each black group, throughout the four-year monitoring period, and for no other ethnic categories at any time.[4] More encouraging news, however, is that all ethnic groups have shared in the fall in permanent exclusions since 1996/97; in fact, the proportionate decrease has been greater for some minority groups than for white pupils. Nevertheless, the decreases have not always been sufficient to change the degree of over-representation that some groups experience. The over-representation of Black Caribbean pupils has fallen from a peak in 1995/96 of 4.7 (that is, Black Caribbean pupils accounted for more than four times the number of exclusions than would be predicted given their size in the school population) to a low of 3.7 in 1998/99. The over-representation of Black African pupils also fell during the same period (from 1.8 to 1.5). Unfortunately, the over-representation of pupils defined as Black Other has worsened during the period (from 2.9 to 3.7).

Exclusions tend to be higher in inner-city areas. As with the attainment inequality discussed above, these findings cannot be solely accounted for by reference to the constitution of separate ethnic groups. It has been noted that African Caribbean children are more likely to live in single-parent households, but rather less attention has been given to the fact that excluded African Caribbeans differ considerably from the profile of other excludees. Specifically, a study by Ofsted reveals that, in comparison with their white counterparts,

'Caribbean' students in their sample were more likely to be described as of 'average or above-average ability', and their 'disruptive behaviour did not usually date from early in their school career, nor was it so obviously associated with deep-seated trauma as with many of the white children' (Ofsted, 1996:11). Additionally, a subsequent inspection revealed that 'the lengths of fixed-period exclusions varied considerably in some schools between black and white pupils for what were described as the same or similar incidents' (Ofsted, 2001:23). A similar disjunction between reported behaviour in school and rates of exclusion has been found for 'looked after' students (Jackson, 2000).

In summary, although there are different ways of relating area to educational outcomes, outcomes in deprived areas are worse than those in non-deprived areas, whether they are measured in terms of qualifications, attendance, exclusions or 'staying on' rates. Inner-city areas in particular feature as having low outcomes. A related pattern of differential experiences and attainment can be identified in relation to minority ethnic students. In the next chapter, we consider the evidence that illuminates the extent to which these differences are attributable to different inputs.

[1] Of all core subjects, performance in English is the most strongly affected by social background variables (Sammons *et al.*, 1997).

[2] The Youth Cohort Study (YCS) uses postal surveys to explore the experiences and attainments of separate groups (cohorts) of 16–19 year olds. The samples are large (usually around 14,000 young people) and nationally representative. The strength of the YCS is its ability to examine the interplay of multiple factors (such as ethnic origin, social class and gender) which are often absent from other surveys. However, considerable caution must be exercised when looking at such analyses because, for example, the relevant sample sizes can shrink dramatically once so many different factors are taken into account simultaneously.

[3] African Caribbean, Bangladeshi and Pakistani young people are significantly less likely to achieve five or more higher grade GCSE passes (Pathak, 2000; Amin *et al.*, 1997; Gillborn and Mirza, 2000).

[4] For any social group, the degree of over-/under-representation can be calculated by taking the percentage of all permanent exclusions that are accounted for by members of the group, and dividing by the percentage of the pupil population which the group makes up. For example, if a group made up 10 per cent of exclusions, but only 5 per cent of the population, it would be over-represented in exclusions by twice the predicted figure (see Gillborn, 1995).

3
Financial and 'real' inputs

This chapter considers the evidence that can be used to illuminate the extent to which the differences in outcomes between schools in deprived and non-deprived areas reported in Chapter 2 might be attributable to differences in inputs. In discussing inputs, it is important to look at 'real' inputs as well as financial inputs. We have included in the former category a range of inputs, including pupil intake, capacity, access and personnel (salaried and 'volunteers').

There is obviously a close and sometimes two-way relationship between financial and 'real' inputs. For instance, the ability to recruit teachers with appropriate experience is dependent on available financial resources. Teachers, in turn, can be effective at generating extra financial inputs through, for example, seeking out private sponsorship. But the real inputs are not only a reflection of financial inputs – they also reflect the capacity of the local context, and it is in this dimension that we can also see a difference between schools in deprived and non-deprived areas.

FINANCIAL INPUTS

The pattern of public spending varies considerably across the country. In their analysis of flows of public expenditure for 1995/96 in three urban areas (Brent, Liverpool and Nottingham), Bramley *et al.* (1998) found different patterns of spending at ward level and between services. They calculate that public spending in the most deprived wards is about 45 per cent above spending in the least deprived wards, but that there was much variation around this overall figure. Some services showed a strong skew towards provision in deprived areas. Education, particularly secondary education, showed a 'relatively flat' pattern of per capita spending and they argued that current patterns of distribution of education spending were less favourable to poor areas.

LEA resources

There is variation across LEAs in the amount of funds they receive from central government through the Standard Spending Assessment.[1] This variation is partly designed to reflect the different degrees of deprivation within, for instance, metropolitan areas and shire counties – although Bramley *et al.*'s (1998) analysis found that DfEE (and Department of Health) programmes displayed less skew towards deprived areas than those of other government departments. London boroughs conventionally receive greater amounts of funds than other urban areas, even though both will contain deprived areas. Bramley *et al.*'s (1998) study, for instance, shows relatively high levels of spending in Brent compared to Liverpool and Nottingham.

Public expenditure at school level is not only determined by the amount of funds received from central government, it also reflects local authorities' resources and distribution priorities. However, since the Local Management of Schools (LMS) policy of 1988 and, more recently, since the Fair Funding framework was introduced in 1999, schools have been given increasing responsibility for managing their own budgets. The distribution of funds from the LEA to individual schools is based on a formula – which is driven mainly by the number and age of pupils.

The age-weighting dimension of the formula funding system can disadvantage schools serving deprived populations, as these are less likely to have sizeable sixth forms. But the formula does also allow LEAs to make some adjustments in recognition of the fact that schools serving deprived populations need additional extra resources. Recent analysis (DfEE, 2000a) shows that the number of LEAs using social deprivation factors to allocate funds has increased over the last three years from 42 in 1996/97 to 61 in 1998/99.[2] The number of students eligible for free school meals is clearly one of the simplest indicators of need built into the formula, but some LEAs offer additional money for other hardships experienced by schools, such as 'pupil turbulence' (see, for instance, Power et al., 1995).

Although the HMI Annual Report (Ofsted, 2000a) notes that most schools are judged to be adequately resourced for teaching the curriculum, it also claims that 'there are unacceptably wide variations in the income that schools receive'. This is the case both for primary and secondary schools. Smith and Noble (1995) report wide variations in the standard spending assessments per pupil at secondary level, ranging from £2,791 per pupil in Bradford to £4,180 per pupil in Hackney (1992 figures). Differences in the LMS formula also mean wide discrepancies within the same LEA both for different age groups and between schools in similar geographical areas. The recent report *Improving City Schools* (Ofsted, 2000b) found that some schools, serving comparable populations, attracted twice as much per-pupil funding as other schools. The report also claims that this variation is more pronounced in disadvantaged areas.

There were concerns when LMS and open enrolment were first introduced that financial resources would be redistributed *away* from schools serving deprived populations. Although these concerns were not justified by the earlier studies of the implementation of LMS, more recent analyses do suggest regressive redistribution. Levačić's (1993) ICOSS (Impact of Competition on Secondary Schools) study of the effects of LMS on 300 secondary schools in six LEAs after its first year of implementation found that the direction of the flow of money varied from LEA to LEA. In general, though, Levačić concludes that schools with higher proportions of socially disadvantaged pupils did not lose out. Bullock and Thomas's (1997) survey of 160 schools over three years found that some schools in deprived areas gained in some LEAs but not in others. However, subsequent analysis of the ICOSS data (Hardman and Levačić, 1997) reveals that over a six-year period one in ten schools had continuously deteriorating pupil recruitment and that these schools were disproportionately attended by pupils entitled to FSM. Levačić's own review of the evidence leads her to conclude that 'some of the more disadvantaged pupils have benefited least or suffered most as a consequence of local management' (1998:346).

Diminishing resource levels are partly due to the difficulty these schools have in attracting pupils (discussed later). But the higher incidence of poverty can be compounded by the extra demands often made on schools serving disadvantaged populations. *Improving City Schools* (Ofsted, 2000b) focuses on schools coming out of special measures and draws attention to the extra expenditure often faced by schools situated in deprived areas. These include:

- security, and paying for results of vandalism and theft
- providing and replacing books and equipment (HMI also pointed out that some schools were finding it difficult to resource the new strategies adequately)
- supporting pupils with SEN or EAL
- subsidising costs of school trips and visits
- tackling disaffection and poor attendance.

The report claims that even when deprived schools do receive extra funds, these are not necessarily sufficient to offset their extra difficulties. As *Improving City Schools* concludes:

> The figures tell us that, whatever funding premium there might be for some schools in disadvantaged areas, it does not produce a bonus in terms of learning resources. (Ofsted, 2000b:45)

Additional private sponsorship

Public-private partnerships have brought extra resources (of cash or in kind) into schools, either through government programmes such as Education Action Zones or through locally organised education-business partnerships. A DfEE survey (1999b) reports that 48 per cent of primary and 92 per cent of secondary schools have some sort of link with business. Public-private partnerships are a feature of a number of recent central government programmes, such as EAZs, designed to target extra resources at schools in deprived areas.

The increasing involvement of private sponsors may bring extra resources into schools but it creates problems in assessing financial and real inputs in order to calculate cost-effectiveness. To date, no recent research studies have systematically attempted to map out the distribution and quantity of the contribution of private sponsors. However, it can be predicted that schools in deprived areas are likely to find fewer sponsors than those in more affluent areas. In 1990, Sumner and Hutchinson found that schools in county towns and rural areas raised twice as much per pupil as inner-city schools. Recent interim research findings on EAZs highlight the uneven distribution and variable contribution of business partners. Amongst the 25 first-wave EAZs, one zone almost tripled their target sponsorship level of £250,000, while another raised less than a sixth of the same expected target (Dickson *et al.*, 2000). In addition, their contributions are dependent on the prevailing economic climate, and in some instances private sponsors have found themselves unable to contribute what they had promised. Finally, these schemes often depend on the commitment of individual members of staff and the partnership fails when the individual moves on (Power *et al.*, 2000).

Assessing the impact of financial inputs in deprived areas

Even despite these problems, schools in deprived areas may receive more financial inputs than schools in non-deprived areas. The fact that the greater financial investment is not reflected in outcomes indicates that the compensatory mechanisms are insufficient. Past research (Mortimore *et al.*, 1988) has shown that disadvantages 'stack up' in a linear way, making it exceedingly difficult for children living in deprived areas to succeed. A more recent review (Whitty *et al.*, 1998) into the intersection of health and education inequalities further highlights the cumulative nature of disadvantage.

The relationship between the scale and kind of financial input and educational outcome is a heavily contested issue. In part, this is because the evidence is limited and ambiguous. In their report to the DfEE, Vignoles *et al.* (2000) claim that international research *does* establish a link between certain inputs (especially expenditure and teacher characteristics) and enhanced student outcomes. The UK literature is more ambiguous, but it too supports the claim that resources have an impact on outcomes. For instance, some of the research that Vignoles *et al.* (2000) review is of direct relevance to this report and reveals the complex relationship between financial input and learning outcome. One relevant example they examine is a quasi-experimental study designed to assess the effectiveness of early literacy programmes aimed at targeted groups of pupils.

Reading Recovery (RR) and alternative Phonological Interventions (PI) (QCA, 1998) were trialled on a sample of 390 six-year-old children from 63 schools in London who had made a slow start with reading. The use of controls for each of the interventions demonstrated that the RR children made significantly greater progress than the control group – but this gap waned after four years. On the other hand, the PI children did not show immediate post-intervention gains in the reading, but made greater gains in both reading (only narrowly missing statistical significance) and spelling after four years. However, RR *did* have a positive and significant lasting impact on reading for two sub-sets of children – those receiving FSM and those not reading at six. Both PI and RR had a significant impact on reading and spelling compared to FSM children in control schools.

This very focused study illustrates the complex relationship between financial input and educational outcome. It shows that the same intervention can have differential effects on different types of students over different periods of time. In this case, targeted investment had a greater beneficial impact on FSM students – those who are likely to be over-represented in schools in deprived areas.

What is clear is that more research needs to be done on the cost-effectiveness of particular educational interventions, and particularly on the extent to which it is better to target extra inputs at individuals rather than at areas (Plewis, 1998).

'REAL' INPUTS

In their outline of the 'ideal research project' needed to unravel the relationship between resource allocation and pupil attainment, Vignoles *et al.* (2000) identify three explanatory variables which need to be considered: the pupil variable, the neighbourhood variable and the school variable. We will consider the school variable in the next chapter when we look at processes and service quality.

The relationship between the pupil and the neighbourhood variable is one of the issues that lie at the heart of this review. Do schools serving deprived areas have outcomes that reflect the aggregated individual attributes of their incoming pupils, or is there a threshold beyond which there is an extra 'area effect'? In addition, are there other aspects of being located in a deprived neighbourhood that influence the pupil intake and then have an impact on outcomes?

The pupil intake
The peer effect

There is some evidence, although it is not very robust, of an 'area' effect over and above aggregated individual attributes where concentrations of disadvantage are high enough. If we refer back to Table 2.3 (page 17), we can see that where schools drew from 'mixed' housing, the outcomes were closer to the higher end than the lower end. Benn and Chitty (1996) use these figures to show that pupil 'mix' has a leavening effect.

However, as we noted earlier, there are problems with these data. Further difficulties with this particular interpretation are that we do not know what proportions make up the 'mix'. It also needs to be noted that both Benn and Chitty are strong supporters of comprehensive schooling.

Arguments about the 'peer effect' have been well aired in the debate about selective versus comprehensive education. Given the volume of research in this area, it is worth revisiting it here to see what it can tell us about the strengths and weaknesses of schools with more homogenous populations. Although the homogeneity in the selection debate relates to test attainment rather than background or locality, the connection between attainment and background is such that grammar schools tend to serve non-deprived populations and secondary moderns tend to serve less privileged populations and localities.

In a recent review of the literature, Crook *et al.* (1999) identify the more reliable studies and conclude that the difference between either system is small. The average output, or 'system productivity', of selective and comprehensive systems is much the same. However, there would appear to be variations at school level which suggest that more able children do better in grammar schools and less able children do better in comprehensive schools. This suggests that greater homogeneity of incoming pupils within schools leads to greater polarisation of outcomes between schools.

What is not clear, even from these more reliable studies, is whether the differences in outcomes are the result of differences in financial inputs and/or of having a more qualified and stable teaching staff. Grammar schools tend to have greater per-pupil income because of the size of their sixth forms, and employ more qualified teaching staff who stay longer (Kerckhoff *et al.*, 1996). Thus the better performance of academically able students in grammar schools may be attributable to the incidental benefits of selection rather than selection itself.

The issue of homogeneity of intake and how it affects schools serving deprived areas has come to the fore recently because of debates about the impact of market-oriented reforms set in train by the Conservative governments. Evidence from qualitative case studies shows that these reforms have contributed to greater polarisation. Gewirtz *et al.* (1995) show schools seeking students who are 'able', 'gifted', 'motivated and committed' and middle class, with girls and children with South Asian backgrounds being seen as particular assets in terms of their potential to enhance test scores. The least desirable clientele include those who are 'less able' and/or have special educational needs, especially emotional and behavioural difficulties, as well as children from working-class backgrounds and boys, unless they also have some of the more desirable attributes. Smith and Noble (1995) conclude from the available evidence that English choice policies are further disadvantaging already disadvantaged groups. Although schools have always been socially and racially segregated to the extent that residential segregation exists, Gewirtz *et al.* (1995) suggest that choice may well exacerbate this segregation by extending it into previously integrated schools serving mixed localities. They argue that working-class children, and particularly children with special educational needs, are increasingly 'ghetto-ised' in schools with falling populations and therefore falling income.

However, the evidence from analyses of larger scale datasets comes to a different conclusion. The broadest study has been conducted by Gorard and Fitz (1998a; 1998b; Fitz and Gorard, 2000), whose findings are drawn from school-level data for all schools in England and Wales, encompassing eight million students in 23,000 schools over ten years. Their analysis suggests that just after the reform, the market system created a slight increase in segregation, which has subsequently settled down and led to a decrease in segregation in most areas. They claim to show that segregation has declined significantly in every region, in both primary and secondary schools, as assessed by the proportions of FSM students, first language, ethnicity, and statements of special educational needs.

Their research has, however, been disputed by several commentators (e.g. Noden, 2000; Gibson and Asthana, 1999). The disputes are mainly methodological: over the use of FSM as an indicator, and the varying indices of segregation that attempt to calculate the levels of social segregation between schools. Part of the difficulty lies in linking local shifts within broader trends. In addition, it is probably too early to say what the long-term effects of recent reforms are.

Pupil turbulence

Another aspect of the peer effect that appears to have a neighbourhood and socio-economic dimension is the amount of pupil mobility in schools in deprived areas. Turnover also has an impact on the ability of the school to make appropriate provision available (see Dobson et al., 2000).

Benn and Chitty (1996) define 'high' turnover as new pupils entering at the rate of at least one per week, with low turnover defined as fewer then ten per year. Nearly half (46 per cent) of the schools in cities had high turnovers, and 29 per cent of schools with predominantly working-class intakes had high rates. Benn and Chitty argue that in connection with turnover, the kind of housing is less important than its quality. Among comprehensive schools drawing pupils from substandard housing, 59 per cent recorded high levels of turnover – significantly more than, for instance, the 29 per cent drawing pupils from council housing.

Dobson et al. (2000) report that very high pupil mobility (over 30 per cent turnover) is particularly associated with armed forces' families, refugees and asylum seekers and low-income families who are in temporary accommodation. High pupil mobility in schools is also strongly associated with social deprivation and is particularly prominent in inner London, other large cities and coastal resorts; in fact, in those areas already identified as containing high concentrations of poverty.

The difficulty of establishing a direct relationship between mobility, attainment and progress is explored by Strand's (2000) analysis of KS1 tests from over 6,000 pupils in an urban education authority. He reports that the impact of mobility itself is low relative to other pupil background factors. However, he also claims that 'the implications of mobility for school and classroom management, planning and resourcing are substantial' and should not be underestimated.

The negative impact on pupils and schools created by the homelessness associated with temporary accommodation in seaside resorts is recorded in a study of primary schools in deprived areas in Portsmouth (Stepien et al., 1996). A report by Her Majesty's Inspectorate (HMI) into the problems which homelessness creates for both students and schools in four areas – Blackpool, Great Yarmouth, Manchester and London (HMI, 1990) – refers to difficulties for pupils in finding places and having restricted access to options within the curriculum. School difficulties included the pressure to accommodate sudden influxes of pupils without additional resources.

Research, some of it from the US (Bassuk and Rosenberg, 1988; Stronge, 1989; Kozol, 1988) shows that, on average, schools with high levels of pupil mobility perform less well than schools with low pupil mobility. Almost all schools with mobility rates over 20 per cent in the postal survey carried out by Dobson et al. (2000) reported that mobility had affected school performance and National Curriculum tests. One of the Northern coastal schools in this survey reported a difference of almost 20 per cent between percentage success rates of Level 4 SAT results (of 50 per cent to almost 70 per cent) if non-routine admissions were excluded from the figures.

There is some evidence of a differentiated effect on performance according to different groups of mobile students. For instance, for schools where mobility is linked to movement of armed forces families, average performance levels are relatively high (Dobson *et al.*, 2000). This group of mobile pupils also have a lower number of pupils eligible for free school meals. According to the case studies on mobile pupils, 10 per cent of the service pupils joining schools were eligible for FSM compared with 76 per cent of mobile pupils in the London case study school (Dobson *et al.*, 2000).

Capacity

Benn and Chitty (1996:201) comment that 'overcrowdedness was associated 30 years ago with poor schools in poor areas, but after the late 1970s when the bulge had passed and numbers began to fall, being "full" began to be associated with success'. Of the schools they surveyed, middle-class ones were far more likely to be full than working-class ones. But this pattern had geographical variations. Rural comprehensives were the least likely to be full – even though they had the best academic results and most middle-class intakes. In addition, a larger proportion of schools in metropolitan areas were full than ones in the shires. On the other hand, 14 per cent of schools claimed to be 'not full' because they were located in run-down or inaccessible areas. Similarly, one-third (34 per cent) of those that were oversubscribed claimed that this was because they were 'in a pleasant neighbourhood'.

Their findings are confirmed by those of Hardman and Levačić (1997), whose case study of a metropolitan area with considerable levels of social deprivation reveals that the proportion of places filled in schools was negatively related to the percentage of socially disadvantaged pupils. Dobson *et al.* (2000) also note that many high-mobility schools have spare places, whereas low-mobility schools tend to recruit from the 'settled' parts of the local population and have few vacancies, sometimes filled by operating waiting lists.

Access

The data on capacity might suggest that those who live in pleasant areas find it harder to gain access to schools than those who live in urban and, in particular, in run-down areas. However, the issue of access is complex as it has to encompass other issues: access to *what quality* of provision; *who* gets access when spaces are limited and the *friction of distance.*

Proximity to schools (as with doctors, shops and banks) is mentioned as one of the access indicators of deprivation (see Noble *et al.*, 1999). However, the friction of distance varies for different groups. For instance, non-deprived areas with no 'local' schools may not be considered educationally deprived, provided access to nearest schools does not involve disproportionate cost and inconvenience. Hence, proximity to schools as an indicator of educational disadvantage becomes applicable when related to other indicators of disadvantage, e.g. car ownership. It may also be a particular problem for poor families in rural locations where public transport is infrequent.

Issues of access related to school admissions also complicate issues of proximity. If local education markets do create segregating effects, then 'local' schools could well become inaccessible to local populations. As the research on social polarisation cited earlier (e.g. Gewirtz *et al.*, 1995) suggests, where there are insufficient places for the number of applicants, processes of selection (both formal and informal) work against parents in deprived areas, even where the school is itself located in such an area.

There is also a geographic dimension to access. Parents are less likely to get the school of their choice in urban areas. This is particularly pronounced in relation to inner London. An Audit Commission survey of parents (1997) found that most parents supported the principles of diversity and choice and wanted access to a range of schools. The extent to which parents do have access to a variety of schools is likely to depend partly on historical and geographical factors, but also on the principles through which places are allocated. There is currently little research on the extent to which a range of potential alternatives are equally available to parents in deprived or non-deprived areas. Research on grant-maintained schools (Fitz *et al.*, 1992) shows that at that time the majority of opted-out schools tended to be in non-deprived rather than deprived areas, but more research needs to be done on the location and accessibility of the 'newer' alternatives, such as specialist schools. Grammar schools are often located in inner-city areas, but while parents in these areas may have formal access, relatively few children from poor homes end up attending them (Crook *et al.*, 1999). For example, of 36,063 parents eligible to vote on the admission policies of three Barnet grammar schools, 23,000 live outside Barnet. Parents with children at only 31 of Barnet's 94 primary schools are eligible to vote (CASE, 2000).

The Audit Commission (1997) survey of parents drawn from five different areas shows the variation in levels of success in gaining preferred options and levels of satisfaction (see Table 3.1, page 43). The socio-economic characteristics of the area and of the sample of parents interviewed can only be inferred. However, the most deprived of these areas is likely to be the one within an inner London borough – where the proportion of 'satisfied' parents is strikingly lower than in the other areas. The findings of the Audit Commission survey are also supported by those of Fitz and Gorard (2000) who claim that appeals are more common in areas with high levels of FSM.

TABLE 3.1 VARIATION IN LEVELS OF SATISFACTION WITH GAINING OPTION CHOICES

	A	B	C	D	E	Overall
% not stating genuine first preference†	17	11	4	4	8	9
% not getting their stated first preference†	32	3	4	5	10	10
Net satisfaction††			+7	+76	+65	+61	+81	+59

†   Excludes those who would have preferred either an independent or selective
    school
†† Percentage 'satisfied' minus percentage 'dissatisfied'

A   Area within an inner-London borough
B   Part of a large metropolitan city
C   Large but sparsely populated in a rural LEA
D   Medium-sized industrial town in an urban county LEA
E   Small city in the South East within a semi-rural LEA

Source: Audit Commission, 1997

Teachers

Teachers are the largest resource cost in education, accounting for 70
per cent of the total school education expenditure in the UK (Mayston
and Jesson, 1999). The House of Commons Select Committee on
Education and Employment (2000) noted regional problems in the
supply of teachers, particularly in inner cities and London. It identified
low morale and low pay as a factor in teacher shortages. A survey of
secondary schools carried out by the Times Educational Supplement
(TES) and the Secondary Heads Association found that there were
more than 1,734 teacher vacancies in the 1,600 schools contacted at
the start of the autumn term 2000 (Dean, 2000). They claim that if
these shortages were replicated across the 3,800 secondary schools
in England and Wales, there would be more than 4,000 vacancies.[3]

The 'crisis' in the supply and retention of teachers became a major concern in the 1990s. This has in the past been seen as a 'London problem'. Chilver (1991) reported annual resignations in Greater London at the 20 per cent level compared with 10 per cent in the North. Straker (1992) suggests that newly qualified teachers (NQTs) are not very geographically mobile, and that it would be difficult to attract teachers to London from elsewhere.[4] Straker suggests that there are likely to be teacher shortages in areas where the cost of living is high (such as London), and in subject areas where jobs are more lucrative outside teaching. The recent report for the Teacher Training Agency by the University of North London (Hutchings, 2000) outlines the difficulties of teacher recruitment and retention, particularly in inner London boroughs. This found that these boroughs are more likely to have a teaching force with a young age profile and have difficulty recruiting head teachers. This study also showed a highly significant correlation between the average number of teacher applications received and a school's GCSE results, indicating greater competition in the secondary sector for places in 'higher' performing schools. This finding was also supported by data derived from interviews with teachers and from qualitative analysis of questionnaires.

Evidence from the TES survey indicates that teacher shortages are not limited to London. Secondary schools in North Yorkshire and the East of England have reported difficulties in filling vacancies for maths and English posts. At least one in five of the vacancies for English teachers advertised for September in the North East, North Yorkshire and the Humber, the West Midlands and the East of England remain unfilled after the start of the autumn term.

As part of the inspection process, Ofsted collect data on the match between teachers' qualifications and the subjects and age range they teach. On the basis of this Ofsted judge that the match of number, qualifications and experience of teachers to the demands of the subject curriculum is 'good' in about six out of ten secondary schools. It is 'unsatisfactory' overall in one secondary school in 20 (Ofsted, 2000a). Other data suggest that schools serving deprived populations are more likely to employ teachers whose qualifications and experience are mismatched to the subject or age range they teach. For instance, Ofsted (1999) reports on the basis of inspection evidence that most of the schools in which the amount of 'good teaching' decreased served areas with above-average levels of disadvantage. They attribute this to the difficulty in recruiting and retaining teachers in these schools.

This difficulty means that these schools are likely to have a greater reliance on supply teachers. The 2000 Annual Report judges that only a quarter of lessons taught by supply teachers was 'satisfactory' (Ofsted, 2000a). Similarly, *Improving City Schools* (Ofsted, 2000b) reports that the quality of teaching both in primary and secondary schools was lower in schools serving disproportionate numbers of students eligible for FSM (more than 35 per cent) than for all schools.

The mismatch between teacher qualifications and subject and age range taught, and the particular problems of teacher recruitment and retention in deprived areas, may well contribute to the poorer performance of schools in these areas. Teacher and support staff characteristics are one of the few areas that can be shown by cost-effectiveness analysis to 'make a difference' (Vignoles *et al.*, 2000; Mortimore *et al.*, 1994).

School governors

The role of governing bodies has become increasingly important over the last two decades, and the skills which governors need have become more sophisticated under LMS.

Research by Scanlon *et al.* (1999) reports that there is a clear association between effective schools and effective governing bodies.

This research finding was based on the results of a large-scale national survey of head teachers, chairs of governors and governors, a small exploratory study of 44 schools and nine case studies of effective governing bodies. However, the direction of the link was impossible to prove (see also Creese and Earley, 1999). Ofsted (2000a) describe the most effective governing bodies as those 'involved in the strategic management of schools, encompassing all aspects of development planning and management of resources'. However, Ofsted also acknowledge that not all schools have governors with an adequate level of financial expertise.

Scanlon *et al.* (1999) found that 45 per cent of schools reported difficulty in recruiting members over the previous 12 months. They found a statistically significant link between catchment area and governor recruitment (Table 3.2), with the percentage of schools experiencing recruitment problems increasing in accordance with the percentage of pupils eligible for FSM. Over three-quarters (76 per cent) of schools with very high proportions of FSM children (over 60 per cent) reported difficulties, compared to less than one-third of schools (29 per cent) with low (10 per cent or less) levels of FSM. As Table 3.2 also shows, schools in areas which had difficulty recruiting governors also had difficulty retaining them.

TABLE 3.2: RECRUITMENT AND RETENTION OF GOVERNORS

Catchment area	Difficulties in recruitment (%)	Difficulties in retention (%)
County town/rural	33	14
Suburban	49	17
Urban/inner city	55	30

Source: Scanlon *et al.*, 1999

In terms of the quality of governors, chairs of governing bodies in inner cities were significantly less likely to be satisfied with their collective skills. Only 39 per cent of heads and chairs of governing bodies with high FSM figures (over 60 per cent FSM) said that they had the correct balance of skills and interests. In addition, the majority of head teachers (76 per cent) and chairs (78 per cent) felt that one of the roles of the governor was to represent the local community. However, this was reported to be difficult in inner-city schools and those with high FSM intakes, though not found to be statistically significant.

The problem of representation in some areas is confirmed by other research. In terms of their socio-economic status, school governors tend to be highly educated, white, and in executive, managerial and professional occupations. A series of National Foundation for Education Research studies, based on surveys of representative samples of governors (NFER, 1990; 1991; 1994), has consistently found that black and Asian communities were under-represented among governors.

Deem *et al.*'s 1995 observation of and interviews with three governing bodies of secondary schools in two LEAs found that governors did not always have the same social characteristics as the student/parent body of the school. This was especially true in schools where students were from less privileged economic backgrounds or from minority ethnic groups. Deem *et al.* also found that parent governors, and women and black governors, noticeably participated less in meetings, suggesting that increasing representation is not in itself a sufficient condition for full participation. They conclude that even in schools with a high proportion of ethnic minority students, the governing bodies tend to be mainly white and not interested in equal opportunities or multicultural education issues.

In summary, although the distribution of funds to and within LEAs is designed to reflect the different degrees of deprivation, there are still differences in the amount of funding that schools serving deprived populations receive. Moreover, research on Local Management of Schools increasingly shows a regressive effect on schools, with high proportions of disadvantaged students.

A number of studies show that pupil intake has a 'compositional effect', suggesting that the concentration of disadvantaged pupils adds further disadvantage. Certainly, the higher level of pupil mobility in deprived areas creates pressures on these schools. Additional difficulties reported in the research are the recruitment and retention of appropriately qualified teachers and governors.

Although the level of any additional resources does not seem to be able to meet the needs of schools in deprived areas, this does not mean that money does not make a difference. The relationship between funding and performance is extremely complex and as yet not sufficiently well explored.

[1] A review of local government finance is currently under way, involving consultation on the *Modernising Local Government Finance* Green Paper released by the DETR in September 2001 and a fundamental review of the Standard Spending Assessment arrangements.

[2] Local government reorganisation has changed the number of LEAs in each of the four years mentioned here from 109 to 150, making it impossible to represent these figures as proportions. Nevertheless, it needs to be noted that they comprise a minority of LEAs – albeit a sizeable minority.

[3] Estimates of the shortage of supply of teachers are hotly contested and largely depend on how 'vacancy' is defined. A survey undertaken in January 2001 by the DfEE suggests that the TES/SHA survey over-represents the number of vacancies. The DfEE survey defines a vacancy as a post that has been advertised but not filled, whereas the SHA employs a looser definition. The DfEE survey (based on returns from LEAs)

indicated 2,580 vacancies in English secondary schools. SHA have subsequently responded by claiming that the DfEE definition is 'too narrow', leading to an *under*-representation of the amount of vacancies. They claim a recent re-survey suggests a comparable January 2001 figure of 10,000 vacancies (SHA, 2001) in England and Wales.

[4] DfEE statistics (2000c) on new entrants to teaching show the relationship between region of initial teacher training and region of service. The majority of new entrants remain 'in region' – although there are geographical differences. In 1999, no new entrants (nursery, primary or secondary) trained in London, the South East and South West of England were working in schools in the North East. There was rather more movement from those training in the North West and North East, although these more mobile students still accounted for a minority. For instance, only 3.4 per cent of those trained in the North East were in service in London nursery, primary and secondary schools.

4
Outputs and processes

It is clear that inputs to schools in deprived areas vary, but it is also clear that this variation cannot account entirely for the differential outcomes reported in Chapter 2. In this chapter we look at the extent to which this differentiation can been explained in terms of school processes and the quality of institutional outputs.

Over the last 30 years, a considerable body of research has been undertaken into the influence of the school on educational performance. Early work by Coleman, Jenks and others (Coleman *et al.*, 1966; Jencks *et al.*, 1972) concludes that family and neighbourhood characteristics have a greater impact on student performance than individual schools. Subsequent research (e.g. Rutter *et al.*, 1979; Mortimore *et al.*, 1988) demonstrates that the outcomes of schooling are not totally determined by intake. For instance, Reynolds and

Packer's (1992) review leads them to claim that between 8–15 per cent variation in pupil performance cannot be accounted for by 'background factors', and Thomas and Mortimore's (1996) analysis of performance in one local authority concludes that the variation in pupils' total examination scores attributable to schools is 10 per cent.

For the purposes of this review, we were interested in exploring the extent to which the organisational attribute varies according to whether a school serves a deprived population.

THE ORGANISATIONAL EFFECTIVENESS OF LEAS

Only a few studies have addressed the issue of regional differences in the size, extent and consistency of school effects or the differential impact of pupil and school background characteristics in different regional, socio-economic and educational policy contexts.

Some research has been undertaken on LEAs in England and Wales by Riley *et al.* (1999). Although it provides useful data on the changing context and roles and responsibilities, these largely comprise perceptions of the LEA contribution to quality and school improvement.

Ofsted inspections of LEAs have also been used to give some indication of organisational effectiveness. Those LEAs that have been identified as having serious weaknesses include some of the poorest areas, such as Bradford, Hackney, Haringey, Liverpool and Southwark. Although Ofsted have given favourable reports on some LEAs serving particularly deprived populations, e.g. Newham, the overall impression is that those with the highest concentrations of deprivation are generally less effective than LEAs in more advantaged areas. As yet, however, no systematic analysis has been undertaken of the reliability and validity of Ofsted inspection data relating to LEAs.

The difficulties of comparing across LEAs is illustrated by Gray *et al.*'s (1990) study of schools in six different LEAs in the UK. Although they found substantial differences between the apparent effectiveness of schools (after controlling for student intake) in these different areas, the conclusions that can be drawn from these comparisons are limited, due to differences in the controls employed for student intake (four LEAs were lacking prior attainment data) and the small size of school samples (30 or fewer schools in five LEAs).

Thomas and Smees (2000) undertook a comparative analysis of secondary school effectiveness across regions using datasets relating to a variety of regions. They found that after controlling for all explanatory (background) factors, there were still clear differences in the extent of variation across schools in different regions. The size of school effects also varied considerably between regions. Within the UK, Lancashire, London and Scotland had similar smaller degrees of variance. By contrast, Jersey had much larger variance. These differences are likely to be attributable to varying degrees of academic selection rather than deprivation – although, as we note in Chapter 3, academic selection does have a bearing on increasing social and academic polarisation.

SCHOOL EFFECTIVENESS
Ofsted inspection grades

Ofsted inspection grades have been used to compare school performance, and the relative performance of schools serving deprived populations can be evaluated through setting these grades against the proportion of students eligible for FSM. Analysis of these data (Thomas, 2000) show that Ofsted inspection grades requiring some or substantial improvement are – in most cases – approximately twice as frequent in schools with high concentrations of economically disadvantaged pupils (more than 50 per cent eligible for FSM) than in other schools.

TABLE 4.1: OFSTED EVALUATIONS OF SCHOOL PERFORMANCE

Area in which some or substantial improvement required	All maintained schools	Schools > 50% FSM
Standards	44%	88%
Quality of education	37%	67%
Climate	20%	40%
Management and efficiency	27%	39%

Source: Thomas, 2000

In terms of the type of deprived areas, analysis of more Ofsted data (cited in Audit Commission, 1997) suggests that institutional ineffectiveness is particularly an urban problem, with 8 per cent of metropolitan and 13 per cent of inner London secondary schools reported as 'being schools in difficulty'.

These findings, though, cannot be considered robust. Ofsted reports are designed for different purposes and cannot be seen as being of equivalent rigour as those 'value added' approaches outlined below. The inspection grades arise from collated subjective judgements and it is possible that schools serving more deprived populations present themselves less effectively, or are more negatively perceived, than those with more affluent populations.

Value added analysis

More robust research into the effectiveness of schools has been provided by 'value added' analyses. The value added concept rests on the assumption that schools add 'value' to the achievement of their pupils. In educational research the concept of value added has developed over the last decade from school effectiveness research literature, although it has been used rather differently in other fields such as economics. It is based on the idea of measuring pupil progress, usually in cognitive outcomes such as reading or mathematics attainment, during a given period of time.

In order to measure progress, baseline and outcome measures are required at the beginning and end of the time period. Of course, as pupils grow older we would expect progress or improvement to be made and average attainment levels to rise. Therefore, researchers use the term 'value added' to refer to the extra value that is added by schools to pupil attainment over and above the progress or improvement that might be expected in a normative sense. Value added measures thus seek to establish whether pupils in some schools make relatively greater or less progress than those in other schools over a specified period of time. The most effective of schools would be those in which pupil progress exceeds expectations.

Thomas (1999) has examined the academic progress of disadvantaged pupils (i.e. those entitled to FSM) in Lancashire LEA. The between-school range in (prior attainment only) value added scores for FSM pupils is approximately -11 to +6 GCSE points. For non-FSM pupils the equivalent figures are -6 to +13 GCSE points. Thomas (1999) also notes that: 'only 22 per cent of schools obtain positive value added scores for pupils entitled to free school meals (FSM), whereas 72 per cent of schools obtain positive scores for non-FSM pupils. Moreover, in 93 per cent of schools FSM pupils make less progress on average than other pupils.'

Strand's 1997 value added analysis of pupil progress during KS1 in Wandsworth LEA provides further evidence of the extent to which schools are differentially effective for advantaged and disadvantaged pupils. He found that pupils entitled to FSM started with lower attainment and fell further behind their peers during the course of KS1. Of particular importance for this review is his finding (Strand, 1997:479) that the composition of a school's intake can have a 'substantial effect on pupils' outcomes over and above the effects associated with individual pupils' prior attainment or background'. Pupils made on average less progress in schools with a high proportion of pupils entitled to FSM.

Researchers have also found evidence of compositional effects in secondary schools linked to levels of attainment and social class background. Pupils of 'average ability' in schools with a relatively high concentration of 'high ability' pupils tended to score 'more highly than comparable pupils in schools where the majority of pupils were of low ability' (Mortimore *et al.*, 1994:328). Similarly, negative effects have been 'related to the concentration of students eligible for free school meals' (Mortimore *et al.*, 1994:328).

ISSUES OF EFFECTIVENESS FOR DIFFERENT SOCIAL GROUPS

School effectiveness research has sometimes been criticised in relation to its treatment of wider social circumstances and factors such as racism and sexism (which cannot be quantified and are often assumed to be covered as a part of the pupil 'background' measure) (see Angus, 1993). It has been claimed that a good deal of school effectiveness research fails to address ethnic diversity at all (Hatcher, 1998). Where ethnicity is taken into account, the numbers involved are often too small for robust findings and there is uncertainty about the interpretations derived from the data (Gillborn and Gipps, 1996; Hatcher and Thomas, 2000). For example, relatively few studies have addressed the question of 'differential effectiveness' in terms of ethnicity, that is, whether certain schools are more or less effective for particular ethnic groups. To date there is no simple answer to this question. Some studies have claimed to find such effects but they have not offered a detailed account of the size of the differences nor do they agree on their significance (see Gillborn and Gipps, 1996).

Qualitative research, undertaken for the DfEE (Blair *et al.*, 1998), sought to identify schools that were particularly successful with students from Caribbean, Pakistani or Bangladeshi ethnic backgrounds. The researchers visited schools which achieved good rates of attainment in GCSEs and served pupils of African Caribbean, Pakistani and Bangladeshi ethnic origin. However, the researchers found that in some cases the minority pupils were achieving significantly below the overall rates of the school, suggesting that the minority ethnic pupils were not enjoying equal opportunities in their supposedly 'effective' schools (Bourne, 1998).

Few studies have considered the possibility of compositional effects related to the ethnic make-up of school populations. To date there is no reliable evidence that the balance of particular ethnic groups in a school has an independent effect on pupil progress (Nuttall and Varlaam, 1990; Gillborn and Gipps, 1996).

Thus the evidence strongly suggests the need for further research on school performance over time and in detail for different student groups, not just in terms of total performance but also at department (or subject) level, as well as in other outcome areas (such as vocational and affective/social), in order to describe the full complexity of school effectiveness. Moreover, the apparent differences in the range and extent of school effects indicate the importance of examining separately regional and national indicators of school effectiveness as well as the educational policies that may underlie any differences observed. Although more work also clearly needs to be done on the extent to which different schools add value, the approach has limits in relation to understanding educational outputs in deprived areas and in addressing a social exclusion agenda.

Value added approaches, which depend on following students through from one stage to another, are difficult to follow in schools with fluid populations. As we saw in Chapter 3, this is likely to be particularly acute in deprived areas, where there are often high levels of pupil migration in general (Dobson *et al.*, 2000) and transience associated with homelessness in particular (Power *et al.*, 1995).

CURRICULUM COVERAGE

There is some evidence to suggest that schools serving disadvantaged populations cover less of the curriculum in each subject. Studies by Plewis (1996) and Gillborn and Youdell (2000) suggest that students attending schools serving disadvantaged areas do not get full access to the curriculum in spite of the National Curriculum.

Plewis (1996) investigated the progress of a cohort of 500 Year 1 pupils at 22 primary schools in inner London – one-third white, a quarter African Caribbean, but relatively homogenous in socio-economic terms in the sense that all the schools in the sample were serving 'rather poor inner-city areas'. His study reveals that African Caribbean boys did particularly badly at mathematics because African Caribbean pupils as a group spent less time doing maths in the classroom than white pupils (15 per cent as opposed to 19 per cent). This pattern was consistent across the schools in the sample.

Plewis argues that teacher decisions about coverage are increasingly influenced by attainment. He argues that his evidence is consistent with what has been called the 'Matthew' effect or how 'the rich get richer'. African Caribbean pupils receive less maths as they progress because they performed less well in the past, so that the gap between the two groups, and particularly in relation to boys, grows. This confirms earlier research conducted by Blatchford *et al.* (1989) who also found that teachers covered less of the curriculum if their expectations of pupils were low.

Plewis concludes that the greater the proportion of African Caribbean pupils in a classroom, the lower the level of curriculum coverage. African Caribbean pupils as a group covered less of the mathematics curriculum in Year 2 because many of them attended those schools where less of the curriculum was covered. However, it is important to note that in any one classroom containing both African Caribbean and white pupils, there was no systematic ethnic difference in the amount of the curriculum covered (Plewis, 1996:143). The extent to which this has an ethnic rather than a socio-economic dimension is again difficult to ascertain. Plewis himself claims that:

> It is important to stress that there is no reason to suppose that the relatively high proportion of African Caribbean pupils in a classroom is in itself a *cause* of low coverage; these classrooms could well have a preponderance of socially and economically disadvantaged pupils, *regardless* of their ethnic background. (Plewis 1996:145; his emphases)

Because of the difficulty of isolating ethnic *and* socio-economic differences within this relatively small and largely homogenous group, the issue of whether differential curriculum coverage is related to racial or more general socio-economic factors remains open to question. Certainly other research studies suggest that the 'race' dimension is important. Plewis's findings add further to the existing literature which suggests that teachers often have systematically lower expectations of black pupils. Mortimore *et al.* (1988) found that 31 per cent of African Caribbean pupils were Band 1 on tests, but were assigned to a lower level (Band 2) by teachers. This only happened to 11.5 per cent of other children (with the exception of those who were 'young for their year'). Support for this position has also been gathered in qualitative studies of primary (Connolly, 1998; Wright, 1992) and secondary schools (Figueroa, 1991; Gillborn, 1990; Mac an Ghaill, 1988; Mirza, 1992; Sewell, 1997).

A recent study of two secondary schools in London (Gillborn and Youdell, 2000) highlights the way that teachers' lower expectations of black students were given institutional weight through the schools' use of 'setting by ability' and the structure of GCSE examinations. Indeed, the authors found that African Caribbean students (regardless of their social class background) and their white peers in receipt of FSM were disproportionately likely to be placed in lower-ranked teaching groups, where a more restricted curriculum is taught. This later translated into a disproportionately high chance of being entered in the Foundation tier for GCSEs, where the highest pass grades are not available regardless of how well a candidate performs.

A small-scale but detailed study (Duffield, 1998) of classroom practices in four Scottish secondary schools, two serving pupils from 'high' socio-economic status (SES) catchment areas and two serving 'low' SES catchment areas, found significant variations in teaching approaches. Duffield found no significant SES related differences in the nature of maths teaching, but there were marked SES related differences in English teaching.

TABLE 4.2: PERCENTAGE OF OBSERVATION TIME IN ENGLISH LESSONS ON SELECTED TASKS

	High SES		Low SES	
	School A	School B	School C	School D
Writing	35	29	41	48
Reading	8	8	19	10
Discussion	17	25	3	6

Source: Duffield, 1998

Duffield reports that low SES schools used more frequent individual writing tasks and more continuous reading in class with less variety of activity within the lesson. There were far greater opportunities for discussion in the high SES schools. Although Schools A and C were both deemed to be 'effective' by their LEA, Duffield argues on the basis of observational data that at the high SES schools, even low achievers were able to be more interactive in their learning. What is less clear from this research is how these differences impact on examination performances.

It also needs to be noted that issues relating to equity of curriculum coverage may well change with the amendments to the National Curriculum. These have involved slimming down the compulsory elements to allow greater flexibility and disapplication at KS4 to facilitate the use of alternative qualifications. These reforms have the potential to provide greater 'matching' of the curriculum with the needs of particular groups of pupils – but they may also increase variations in the amount of curriculum covered.

HOME-SCHOOL LIAISON

Good home-school relationships are generally seen as an important factor in promoting educational achievement. Often these relationships are seen to depend on the attributes of the parent body, which would place this discussion in Chapter 3. However, it is just as likely that the strength of the relationship depends on the quality of the home-school liaison policy and practices developed by the school.

A questionnaire survey (Clark and Power, 1998) of the reporting practices of 183 secondary schools found an area-based variation in the frequency with which various schools reported to parents. Area type was identified by the school, so the cautions that applied to Benn and Chitty's (1996) survey need to be borne in mind about the accuracy of the designations here. As Table 4.3 reveals, schools in inner-city areas, which are most likely to include deprived areas, report less frequently to parents than those in suburban and rural areas.

TABLE 4.3: FREQUENCY OF SECONDARY SCHOOL REPORTING ACCORDING TO TYPE

	Once a year	More than once a year
Inner city	53%	47%
Mixed city	44%	56%
Rural	34%	66%
Mixed rural	38%	63%
Town	46%	54%
Suburban	41%	59%

Source: Clark and Power, 1998

This research also showed that the catchment area of the schools was reflected in attendance at parents' evenings. Attendance in inner-city areas is at least 10 per cent lower for each year group than that of the sample as a whole, with average estimated attendance figures for Years 7, 9 and 11 of 69 per cent, 62 per cent and 58 per cent respectively. Rani Puri (1997) reports a 2 per cent attendance at parents' evenings in one inner-city school.

Attendance also declines as pupils progress through the school. The most serious drop found in the Clark and Power survey was over 50 per cent, recorded by an inner-city comprehensive school where numbers were estimated as falling from more than four-fifths (85 per cent) to less than a third (30 per cent). Schools also commented on the different attendance rates between different groups of parents at these events. According to schools, the most significantly under-represented parents came from lower socio-economic groups.

The survey reveals that very few schools in inner-city areas made any special provisions for liaising with their parent populations. Only 8 per cent of the sample as a whole translated reports for parents who had little English. Most of these schools served inner-city catchment areas, but there was also a significant number of schools in these areas, some of which had up to 50 per cent of EAL students, where no special provision was available.

Parents with little or no English reported little understanding of the structure or content of school reports. None of those interviewed had received reports translated into their home language and tended to use family members and friends to help. Parent-teacher consultations presented particular problems for parents with little or no English. Although schools offered the opportunity of alternative arrangements to see teachers, for many parents, particularly working-class and minority ethnic parents, the idea of availing themselves of these was daunting.

SPECIAL PROVISION

The quality of services schools offer depends not just on a uniform entitlement but also on the extent to which they make special provisions available for the particular characteristics of their client group. Special provision for EAL children and their parents is likely to be particularly important in some deprived areas. In Benn and Chitty's (1996) survey, 16 per cent of schools reported that over 5 per cent of their students were 'without' English, 2.6 per cent report having over 30 per cent without English and a further 2.6 per cent report having over 50 per cent. Many of these were situated in areas of social deprivation, with nearly half drawing from substandard housing. A quarter of schools with concentrations at 31 per cent or over were in large cities.

It is frequently believed that overall attainments will be lowered by high concentrations of pupils for whom English is an additional language (see, for example, the case discussed in Vincent, 1992). There is no reliable evidence to support this. Clearly, students with low levels of English language fluency require additional resources and support, but the best available data suggest that once they have attained a reasonable level of fluency, such students are likely to perform at least as well, if not better than their monolingual peers (Gillborn, 1998).

In summary, the research evidence suggests that schools serving deprived populations are less effective than those serving advantaged populations. There is little conclusive data on organisational effectiveness at LEA level, but there is fairly solid and cumulative evidence that schools with concentrations of disadvantaged students do less well than might be expected. Explanations for this vary. Qualitative data based on classroom observation and teacher surveys suggest that schools serving deprived students offer less curriculum coverage and different educational experiences. They also appear to have less frequent and productive liaison with parents and few special provisions to meet the particular needs of the populations they serve.

5
Conclusion and discussion

The purpose of this review has been to examine the available literature and data in order to identify what – if any – hard evidence exists about the performance of mainstream public sector education services in deprived areas compared to non-deprived areas.

The research evidence demonstrates that outcomes of schools serving deprived populations are worse than those of schools serving non-deprived populations. Moreover, during the 1990s, the gap in outcomes grew rather than narrowed. In particular, inner-city areas and students from some minority ethnic groups feature as having low outcomes.

In explaining the variation in performance, research shows that both context-related 'inputs' and organisational factors are important. In relation to inputs, there are still variations in the funds that schools serving similarly deprived populations receive. Differences in resource levels are also likely to have been exacerbated by the increasing amounts of private and business resources being drawn in to schools. An issue here is that we simply do not know the scale and distribution of these resources.

At this point in time not enough is known about the cost-effectiveness of various interventions in order to assess where additional resources might best be invested. The issue of whether area-based funding programmes are more effective for schools serving deprived areas than those driven by formulae based on aggregated individual attributes (Smith, 1999) has yet to be resolved.

Improving recruitment and retention of appropriately qualified teachers would almost certainly help schools in some deprived areas, and it is hoped that government schemes designed to encourage this will pay off. More proactive attempts to recruit and retain school governors from the communities that these schools serve might also be beneficial.

Other strategies to help schools in deprived areas might involve reducing the compositional effects that appear to result from high concentrations of disadvantaged students. One possibility is to try to generate more heterogeneous school intakes – both in terms of academic and socio-economic attributes. Initiatives such as the 'gifted and talented' element of *Excellence in Cities* (DfEE, 1999a), if carefully handled, could represent one step in this direction. More interventionist schemes, such as the 'bussing' operated in the States, might be effective. However, it is unlikely that this kind of scheme would be feasible even if it were desirable.

One area for concern that the review has noted is variation in curriculum coverage. Despite the National Curriculum, it would still seem that those most in need of extra coverage and support do not always receive it. It is too early to say whether the recent flexibilities introduced at Key Stage 4 will improve curriculum provision in schools serving deprived populations. Research evidence has shown, however, that schools serving deprived populations could do more to ensure better home-school relations, which appear to be less facilitative than those in schools serving non-deprived areas.

As noted in the introduction, the last decades have seen increasing attention being paid to the internal dimensions of school improvement, and there is little doubt that education performance has improved as a result. However, if the gap between schools serving deprived areas and those serving non-deprived areas is to narrow, there needs to be differential rates of improvement. Very recent DfEE data suggest that this may be starting to happen. If this is the case, it is to be hoped that this trend continues.

REFERENCES

Ainley, P., Watson, J., Smith, D. and Yeomans, D. (1999), *New Learning Pathways: Participation and progression in PCE&T.* Paper presented at the British Education Research Association, Brighton, September 1999.

Amin, K., Drew, D., Fosam, B. and Gillborn, D. with Demack, S. (1997), *Black and Ethnic Minority Young People and Educational Disadvantage.* London: Runnymede Trust.

Angus, L. (1993), 'The Sociology of School Effectiveness'. *British Journal of Sociology of Education,* 14 (3), 333–45.

Audit Commission (1997), *Trading Places: The supply and allocation of school places.* London: Audit Commission.

Bassuk, E. and Rosenberg, L. (1988), 'Why Does Family Homelessness Occur? A case-control study'. *American Journal of Public Health,* 78, 783–788.

Beckett, F. (2000), 'Couldn't Do Better'. *Guardian Education,* 19 September 2000.

Benn, C. and Chitty, C. (1996), *Thirty Years On: Is comprehensive education alive and well or struggling to survive?* London: David Fulton.

Berthoud, R. (1998), *The Incomes of Ethnic Minorities.* ISER Report 98-1. Colchester: Institute for Social and Economic Research, University of Essex.

— (1999), *Young Caribbean Men and the Labour Market: A comparison with other ethnic groups.* York: YPS for the Joseph Rowntree Foundation.

Blair, M. and Bourne, J. with Coffin, C., Creese, A. and Kenner, C. (1998), *Making the Difference: Teaching and learning strategies in successful multi-ethnic schools.* London: Department for Education and Employment.

Blatchford, P., Burke, J., Farquhar, C., Plewis, I. and Tizard, B. (1989), 'Teacher Expectations in Infant School: Associations with attainment and progress, curriculum coverage and classroom interaction'. *British Journal of Educational Psychology,* 59, 19–30.

Bourne, J. (1998), *Identifying 'Successful' Multi-Ethnic Schools: A plea for effective ethnic monitoring of attainment.* Paper presented at the QCA

Research Symposium on Underachievement, London, 11 June 1998.

Bramley, G., Evans, M., Atkins, J. *et al.* (1998), *Where Does Public Spending Go? A pilot study to analyse the flows of public expenditure to local areas.* London: Department of Environment, Transport and Regions.

Bullock, A. and Thomas, H. (1997), *Schools at the Centre? A study of decentralization.* London: Routledge.

CASE (2000), *Say No to Selection.* CASE newsletter, 36.

Casey, B. and Smith, D. (1995), *Truancy and Youth Transitions.* England and Wales Youth Cohort Study. Research Series: Youth Cohort Report, 34. London: DfEE.

Chahal, K. (2000), *Ethnic Diversity, Neighbourhoods and Housing.* York: Joseph Rowntree Foundation.

Cheng, Y. (1995), *Staying On in Full-Time Education After 16: Do schools make a difference?* England and Wales Youth Cohort Study, Research Series: Youth Cohort Report, 37. London: Policy Studies Institute.

Chilver Report (1991), *4ᵗʰ Report of the Interim Advisory Committee on Teachers' Pay and Conditions.* London: HMSO.

Clark, A. and Power, S. (1998), *Could Do Better: School reports and parents' evenings. A study of secondary school practice.* London: RISE.

Coleman, J.S., Campbell, E.Q., Hobson, C.J., McPartland, J., Mood, A.M., Weinfield, F.D. and York, R.L. (1966), *Inequality of Educational Opportunity.* New York: Arno Press.

Connolly, P. (1998), *Racism, Gender Identities and Young Children: Social relations in a multi-ethnic, inner-city primary school.* London: Routledge.

Creemers, B.P.M., Reynolds, D. and Swint, F.E. (1994), *The International School Effectiveness Research Programme ISERP First Results of the Quantitative Study.* Paper presented at the British Education Research Association conference, Oxford, September 1994.

Creese, M. and Earley, P. (1999), *Improving Schools and Governing Bodies: Making a difference.* London: Routledge.

Crook, D., Power, S. and Whitty, G. (1999), *The Grammar School Question: A review of research on comprehensive and selective education.* London: Institute of Education, University of London.

Dean, C. (2000), 'Four Thousand Teacher Jobs Cannot Be Filled'. *TES,* 8 September 2000.

Deem, R., Brehony, K. and Heath, D. (1995), *Active Citizenship and the Governing of Schools*. Buckingham: Open University Press.

Demack, S., Drew, D. and Grimsley, M. (2000), 'Minding the Gap: Ethnic, gender and social class differences in attainment at 16 (1988–95)'. *Race Ethnicity & Education*, 3 (2), 117–143.

DETR (1998), *Index of Deprivation*. London: DETR.

— (2000), *Indices of Deprivation*. London: DETR.

DfEE (1997), *Excellence in Schools*. London: The Stationery Office.

— (1999a), *Excellence in Cities*. London: DfEE.

— (1999b), *Survey of School Business Links in England 1997/1998*. London: The Stationery Office.

— (1999c), *Permanent Exclusions from Schools in England 1997/98 and Exclusion Appeals Lodged by Parents in England 1997/98*. Statistical First Release, SFR 11/1999. London: DfEE.

— (1999d), *Ethnic Minority Pupils and Pupils for whom English is an Additional Language 1996/97*. Statistical Bulletin, 3/99. London: DfEE.

— (2000a), *Schools Plus: Building learning communities*. A report from the Schools Plus Policy Action Team. London: DfEE.

— (2000b), 'Inner-City Schools Improve Faster to Narrow the Literacy and Numeracy Gap as Test Results Confirm Government Target'. DfEE press release, 20 September 2000.

— (2000c), *Statistics of Education: Teachers England and Wales*. London: DfEE.

— (2000d), *Permanent Exclusions from Schools and Exclusion Appeals Lodged by Parents in England 1998/9 (provisional)*. London: DfEE.

— (2001), 'Teachers in Service and Teacher Vacancies: January 2001 (provisional)'. Statistical First Release, SFR 16/2001 London: DfEE.

Dickson, M., Gewirtz, S., Halpin, D., Power, S. and Whitty, G. (2000), *A 'Third Way' for Education? Early lessons from the English Education Action Zones initiative*. Paper presented at the European Conference on Education Research, Edinburgh, 20–23 September 2000.

Dobson, J., Henthorne, K. and Lynas, Z. (2000), *Pupil Mobility in Schools. Final report*. London: Migration Research Unit, University College London.

Drew, D. (1995), *'Race', Education and Work: The statistics of inequality.* Aldershot: Avebury.

Drew, D., Gray, J. and Sime, N. (1992), *Against the Odds: The education and labour market experiences of black young people.* England and Wales Youth Cohort Study, Report R&D, 68. Sheffield: Employment Department.

Duffield, J. (1998), 'Learning Experiences, Effective Schools and Social Context'. *Support for Learning,* 13 (1), 3–7.

Figueroa, P. (1991), *Education and the Social Construction of 'Race'.* London: Routledge.

Fitz, J. and Gorard, S. (2000), *School Choice and SES Stratification of Schools: New findings from England and Wales.* Paper presented at AERA, New Orleans, 24–28 April 2000.

Fitz, J., Halpin, D. and Power, S. (1992), *Opting for Grant Maintained Status: A study of policy making in education.* End of award report to the ESRC.

Gewirtz, S., Ball, S.J. and Bowe, R. (1995), *Markets, Choice and Equity in Education.* Milton Keynes: Open University Press.

Gibson, A. and Asthana, S. (1999), *Schools, Markets and Equity: Access to secondary education in England and Wales.* Paper presented at the American Education Research Association Annual Conference, Montreal, Canada.

Gillborn, D. (1990), *'Race', Ethnicity and Education: Teaching and learning in multi-ethnic schools.* London: Unwin Hyman.

— (1995), *Racism and Anti-Racism in Real Schools: Theory, policy, practice.* Buckingham: Open University Press.

— (1998), 'Racism, Selection, Poverty and Parents'. *Journal of Education Policy,* 13 (6), 717–735.

Gillborn, D. and Gipps, C. (1996), *Recent Research on the Attainment of Ethnic Minority Pupils.* Report for Ofsted. London: HMSO.

Gillborn, D. and Mirza, H.S. (2000), *Educational Inequality: Mapping race, class and gender – a synthesis of research evidence.* London: Ofsted.

Gillborn, D. and Youdell, D. (2000), *Rationing Education: Policy, practice, reform and equity.* Buckingham: Open University Press.

Gorard, S. and Fitz, J. (1998a), 'Under Starter's Orders: The established market, the Cardiff Study and the Smithfield Project'. *International Studies in Sociology of Education*, 8 (3), 299–314.

— (1998b), 'The More Things Change ... The missing impact of marketisation'. *British Journal of Sociology of Education*, 19 (3), 365–376.

Gray, J., Jesson, D. and Sime, N. (1990), 'Estimating Differences in the Examination Performance of Secondary Schools in Six LEAs: A multilevel approach to school effectiveness'. *Oxford Review of Education*, 16 (2), 137–158.

Gray, J. and Wilcox, B. (1995), *Good School, Bad School: Evaluating performance and encouraging improvement*. Buckingham: Open University Press.

Green, A. (1996), 'Aspects of the Changing Geography of Poverty and Wealth', in J. Hills (ed), *New Inequalities: The changing distribution of income and wealth in the United Kingdom*. Cambridge: Cambridge University Press.

Hardman, J. and Levačić, R. (1997), 'Impact of Competition on Secondary Schools', in R. Glatter, P. Woods and C. Bagley (eds), *Choice and Diversity in Schooling: Perspectives and prospects*. London: Routledge.

Hatcher, R. (1998), 'Social Justice and the Politics of School Effectiveness and Improvement'. *Race Ethnicity and Education*, 1 (2), 267–289.

Hatcher, R. and Thomas, S. (2000), 'Debate: Equity and school effectiveness research'. *Race Ethnicity and Education*, 3 (1), 103–109.

HEFCE (1997), *The Influence of Neighbourhood Type on Participation in Higher Education*. HEFCE Interim Report 1997. London: HEFCE.

Hills, J. (ed.) (1996), *New Inequalities: The changing distribution of income and wealth in the United Kingdom*. Cambridge: Cambridge University Press.

HMI (1990), *A Survey of the Education of Children Living in Temporary Accommodation*. London: Department of Education and Science.

House of Commons Select Committee on Education and Employment (2000), *Sixth Report: Standards and Quality in Education: The Annual Report of Her Majesty's Chief Inspector of Schools 1998–99* (paragraph b). London: Stationery Office.

Hutchings, M., Menter, I., Ross, A., and Thomson, D. with Bedford, D. (2000), *Teacher Supply and Retention in London 1998–99: A study of six London boroughs*. London: TTA.

Jackson, S. (2000), 'Promoting the Educational Achievement of Looked-After Children', in T. Cox (ed.), *Combating Educational Disadvantage*. London: Falmer Press.

Jencks, C., Smith, M., Acland, H., Bane, M., Cohen, D., Gintis, H., Heyns, B. and Michelson, S. (1972), *Inequality: A reassessment of the effect of family and schooling in America*. New York: Basic Books.

Kerckhoff, A.C., Fogelman, K., Crook, D. and Reeder, D. (1996), *Going Comprehensive in England and Wales: A study of uneven change*. London: Woburn Press.

Kozol, J. (1988), *Rachel and her Children: Homeless families in America*. New York: Crown.

Levačić, R. (1993), 'Assessing the Impact of Formula Funding on Schools'. *Oxford Review of Education*, 19 (4), 435–457.

— (1998) 'Local Management of Schools in England: Results after six years'. *Journal of Education Policy*, 13 (3), 331–350.

— (2000), *Working Paper on Cost-Effectiveness Analysis*. Unpublished.

Mac an Ghaill, M. (1988), *Young, Gifted and Black: Student-teacher relations in the schooling of black youth*. Milton Keynes: Open University Press.

Mayston, D. and Jesson, D. (1999), *Linking Educational Resourcing with Enhanced Educational Outcomes*. Interim Research Report RR179 to the DfEE. London: HMSO.

McCallum, I. and Redhead, G. (1998), 'Demography and School Performance'. *BURISA*, 135, 2–6.

— (2000), 'Poverty and Educational Performance'. *Poverty*, 106, 14–17.

Mirza, H.S. (1992), *Young, Female and Black*. London: Routledge.

Modood, T., Berthoud, R., Lakey, J., Nazroo, J., Smith, P., Virdee, S. and Beishon, S. (1997), *Ethnic Minorities in Britain: Diversity and disadvantage*. London: Policy Studies Institute.

Modood, T. and Shiner, M. (1994), *Ethnic Minorities and Higher Education: Why are there differential rates of entry?* London: Policy Studies Institute.

Morris, E. (2000), 'Morris Announces Good Progress with EAZs'. DfEE press release, 22 March 2000.

Mortimore, P. and Mortimore, J. (1999), *Protecting At-Risk Youth from Educational Failure*. Paper presented at Preparing Youth for the 21st

Century: The transition from education to the labour market, OECD Conference, Washington DC, USA, 23–24 February 1999.

Mortimore, P., Mortimore, J. and Thomas, H. (1994), *Managing Associate Staff.* London: Paul Chapman.

Mortimore, P., Sammons, P., Stoll, L., Lewis, D., and Ecob, R. (1988), *School Matters: The junior years.* Wells: Open Books.

Mortimore, P. and Whitty, G. (1999), 'Can School Improvement Overcome the Effects of Disadvantage?', in T. Cox (ed.), *Combating Educational Disadvantage.* London: Falmer Press.

NFER (1990), *A Survey of School Governing Bodies.* Report by W. Keys and C. Fernandes for the NFER. Slough: NFER.

— (1991), *Towards Effective Partnerships in School Governance.* Report by M. Baginski *et al.* for the NFER. Slough: NFER.

— (1994), *School Governing Bodies: Making progress?* Report by P. Earley for the NFER. Slough: NFER.

Noble, M., Penhale, B., Smith, G. and Wright, G. (1999), *Measuring Multiple Deprivation at the Local Level.* Report by the Social Disadvantage Research Group. Oxford: University of Oxford.

Noden, P. (2000), *Rediscovering the Impact of Marketisation: Dimensions of social segregation in England's secondary schools 1997–99.* Paper presented at the Parental Choice and Market Forces Seminar, King's College, London, 25 February 2000.

Nuttall, D. and Varlaam, A. (1990), *Differences in Examination Performance.* RS 1277/90. London: Inner London Education Authority Research and Statistics Branch.

O'Donoghue, C., Thomas, S., Goldstein, H. and Knight, T. (1997), *1996 DfEE study of Value Added for 16-18 Year Olds in England.* London: HMSO.

Ofsted (1996), *Exclusions from Secondary Schools 1995/6.* London: Ofsted.

— (1999), *Annual Report of Her Majesty's Chief Inspector of Schools: Standards and quality in education 1997–1998.* London: Ofsted.

— (2000a), *Annual Report of Her Majesty's Chief Inspector of Schools: Standards and Quality in Education 1998–1999.* London: Ofsted.

— (2000b), *Improving City Schools.* London: Ofsted.

— (2000c), *National Summary Data Report for Secondary Schools.* London: Ofsted.

— (2001), *Improving Attendance and Behaviour in Secondary Schools*. London: Ofsted.

ONS (2000), *Social Inequalities 2000*. London: HMSO.

Pathak, S. (2000), *Race Research for the Future: Ethnicity in education, training and the labour market*. Research Topic Paper RTP01. Nottingham: DfEE Publications.

Payne, J. (1995), *Routes Beyond Compulsory Schooling*. England and Wales Youth Cohort Report, 31. London: Policy Studies Institute.

— (1998), *Routes at 16: Trends and choices in the nineties. An analysis of data from England and Wales*. England and Wales Youth Cohort Study, Research Series: Youth Cohort Report, 55. London: DfEE.

Peach, C. (1996), *Does Britain have Ghettos?* London: Transactions of the Institute of British Geographers, NS 21.

Pennell, H. and West, A. (1995), *Changing Schools: Secondary schools' admissions policies in inner London in 1995*. Clare Market Papers, 9. London: London School of Economics and Political Science.

Plewis, I. (1996), 'Inequalities and the National Curriculum', in B. Bernstein and J. Brannen (eds), *Children, Research and Policy*. London: Taylor and Francis.

— (1998), 'Inequalities, Targets and Zones'. *New Economy*, 1, 104–109.

Plowden Committee (1967), *Children and their Primary Schools: A report of the Central Advisory Council for Education*. London: HMSO.

Power, S. (1997), 'Not Drowning but Waving? Comprehensive education in the 1990s'. *British Journal of Sociology of Education*, 18 (3).

Power, S., Whitty, G., Gewirtz, S., Halpin, D. and Dickson, M. (2000), '*Paving a Third Way?' A policy trajectory analysis of education action zones*. Interim report to the ESRC.

Power, S., Whitty, G. and Youdell, D. (1995), *Education and Homelessness*. London: Shelter.

QCA (1998), *The Long-Term Effects of Two Interventions for Children with Learning Difficulties*. London: QCA.

Rani Puri, S. (1997), 'Working with Parents in a Multicultural Secondary School', in J. Bastiani (ed.), *Home-School Work in Multicultural Settings*. London: David Fulton.

Reynolds, D. and Packer, A. (1992), 'School Effectiveness and School Improvement in the 1990s', in D. Reynolds and P. Cuttance (eds), *School Effectiveness: Research, policy and practice*. London: Cassell.

Riley, K., Docking, J. and Roules, D. (1999), 'Can Local Education Authorities Make a Difference? The perceptions of users and providers. *Educational Management and Administration*, 27 (1), 29–44.

Rutter, M., Maughan, B. and Ouston, J. (1979), *Fifteen Thousand Hours*. Shepton Mallet: Open Books.

Sammons, P., Hillman, J. and Mortimore, P. (1995), *Key Characteristics of Effective Schools: A review of school effectiveness research*. London: Ofsted and Institute of Education, University of London.

Sammons, P., Thomas, S., Mortimore, P., Owen, C. and Pennell, H. (1994), *Assessing School Effectiveness: Developing measures to put school performance in context*. London: Ofsted.

Sammons, P., West, A. and Hind, A. (1997), 'Accounting for Variations in Pupils' Attainment at the End of KS1'. *British Educational Research Journal*, 23 (4), 489–511.

Scanlon, M., Earley, P. and Evans, J. (1999), *Improving the Effectiveness of School Governing Bodies*. Report to the DfEE.

Scheerens, J. (1990), 'School Effectiveness Research and the Development of Process Indicators of School Functioning'. *School Effectiveness and School Improvement*, 1 (1), 61–80.

SEU (1998a), *Bringing Britain Together*. London: Stationery Office.

— (1998b), *Truancy and School Exclusion*. London: Stationery Office

— (1999), *Bridging the Gap: New opportunities for 16–18 year olds not in education, employment or training*. CM 4405. London: Stationery Office.

Sewell, T. (1997), *Black Masculinities and Schooling: How black boys survive modern schooling*. Stoke-on-Trent: Trentham.

SHA (2001), 'Secondary Heads Criticise Government for Underplaying Crisis in Teacher Supply'. SHA press release, 20 April 2001.

Smith, G. (1987), 'Whatever Happened to Educational Priority Areas?' *Oxford Review of Education*, 13 (1), 23–38.

Smith, G., Smith, T. and Wright, G. (1997), 'Poverty and Schooling: Choice, diversity or division?', in A. Walker and C. Walker (eds), *Britain Divided:*

The growth of social exclusion in the 1980s and 1990s. London: Child Poverty Action Group.

Smith, G.R. (1999), *Area-Based Initiatives: The rationale and options for area targeting*. CASE papers, 25. London: CASE, London School of Economics.

Smith, T. and Noble, M. (1995), *Education Divides: Poverty and schooling in the 1990s*. London: Child Poverty Action Group.

Sparkes, J. (1999), *Schools, Education and Social Exclusion*. CASE Papers, 29. London: Centre for Analysis of Social Exclusion, London School of Economics, University of London.

Stepien, D., Lawrence, B., Murray, L. and Clark, A. (1996), *Homelessness, Schooling and Attainment: An interim report*. Portsmouth: University of Portsmouth.

Straker, N. (1991), 'Teacher Supply in the 1990s: An analysis of current developments', in G. Grace and M. Lawn (eds), *Teacher Supply and Teacher Quality*. Clevedon: Multilingual Matters.

Strand, S. (1997), 'Pupil Progress During Key Stage 1: A value added analysis of school effects'. *British Educational Research Journal*, 23 (4), 471–487.

Strand, S. (2000), *Pupil Mobility, Attainment and Progress During Key Stage 1: A study in cautious interpretation*. Paper presented at the Annual Conference of the British Educational Research Association, University of Cardiff, 5–9 September 2000.

Stronge, J.H. (1989), 'Academic Performance of Homeless Children'. Unpublished raw data quoted in Stronge, J. H. (1992), 'The Background: History and problems of schooling for the homeless', in J. H. Stronge (ed.), *Educating Homeless Children and Adolescents: Evaluating policy and practice*. Newbury Park, USA: Sage Publications.

Sumner, R. and Hutchinson, D. (1990), *Resources in Primary Schools*. Slough: NFER.

Thomas, S. (1999), *Optimal Multilevel Models of School Effectiveness: Comparative analysis across regions*. End of award report for ESRC.

— (2000), *Overall Patterns of Achievement*. Working paper on school effectiveness. Unpublished.

Thomas, S. and Mortimore, P. (1996), 'Comparison of Value Added Models for Secondary School Effectiveness'. *Research Papers in Education*, 11 (1), 279–295.

Thomas, S. and Smees, R. (1998), *Dimensions of Secondary School Effectiveness: Comparing the findings from four academic studies.* Paper presented at the annual conference of the American Educational Research Association, San Diego, 13–17 April 1998.

— (2000), *Dimensions of Secondary School Effectiveness: Comparative analyses across regions.* Paper presented at the American Educational Research Association conference, New Orleans, 24–28 April 2000.

Vignoles, A., Levačić, R., Walker, J., Machin, S. and Reynolds, D. (2000), 'The Relationship Between Resource Allocation and Pupil Attainment: A review'. Report for the DfEE. DfEE: London.

Vincent, C. (1992), 'Tolerating Intolerance? Parental choice and race relations – the Cleveland case'. *Journal of Education Policy,* 7 (5), 429–443.

Whitty, G., Aggleton, P., Gamarnikow, E. and Tyler, P. (1998), *Education and Health Inequalities.* Input Paper, 10 to the Independent Enquiry into Inequalities in Health.

Wright, C. (1992), *Race Relations in the Primary School.* London: David Fulton Publishers.

Appendices

APPENDIX 1
RESEARCH STRATEGY

The review of literature for this report required the use of a wide range of academic and organisational electronic databases. A proforma was devised to collect and assess information for the review and datasets (see Appendix 2).

- The following electronic sources were searched:

  The Audit Commission
  DfEE and DfEE analytical services
  Department for the Environment
  Transport and the Regions
  Economic and Social Research Council
  Further Education Funding Council
  Higher Education Funding Council
  Joseph Rowntree Foundation
  National Foundation for Educational Research
  Office for National Statistics
  Office for Standards in Education
  Social Exclusion Unit
  Teacher Training Agency
  Training Standards Council

- Academic electronic databases included the British Education Index and ERIC.

The following list is an example, rather than an exhaustive list of subject headings used to search for data using the BEI. This demonstrates the breadth of material covered in order to reveal material focusing on issues relating to education in deprived and non-deprived areas:

Social deprivation; socio-economic influences; socio-economic status; academic achievement; school meals; value added methods; access to education; social class; equal education; school effectiveness; low achievement; social environment; urban; poverty; educational disadvantaged; education planning; disadvantaged; geographic location; drop-out.

- In addition to these electronic sources, searches were made of paper sources in the following academic and organisational libraries:

Birkbeck College
British Library of Economic and Political Science
Institute of Education
King's College London
University College London
London and Family Policy Studies Institute

- The reviewers were also given access to unpublished research papers by members of the Institute of Education.

- The following web pages were included in the searches.

Joseph Rowntree Foundation:
http://www.jrf.org.uk/knowledge/findings/
http://www.jrf.org.uk/knowledge/wip/(Research in Progress)

ESRC:
http://www.regard.ac.uk/regard/home/index_html?

NFER:
http://www.nfer.ac.uk/cgi-bin/expiscor

Ofsted:
http://www.ofsted.gov.uk
http://www.official-documents.co.uk/document/hoc/157/157-00.htm

DfEE Research Briefs:
http://www.dfee.gov.uk/research/rb_20.htm
http://www.dfee.gov.uk/research/rb_99.htm
http://www.dfee.gov.uk/research/rb_98.htm

DfEE Statistics:
http://www.dfee.gov.uk/statistics/DB/VOL/v0111/2710751.pdf
(Education and Training Statistics 1999)
http://www.dfee.gov.uk/statistics/DB/VOL/v0131/10506.pdf
(Education and Training Statistics 1998)
http://www.dfee.gov.uk/statistics/DB/SBU/b0057/10700e.pdf
(Education and Training Expenditure since 1989/90)
http://www.dfee.gov.uk/statistics/DB/SFR/s0174/sfr30-2000.pdf
(Admission Appeals for Maintained Primary and Secondary Schools
in England 1998/99)
http://www.dfee.gov.uk/statistics/DB/SFR/s0032/sfr-1999.pdf
(Admission Appeals for Maintained Primary and Secondary Schools
by Local Education Authority Area In England 1997/98)
http://www.dfee.gov.uk/statistics/DB/SFR/s0029/sfr-1599.pdf
(Minority Ethnic Pupils in Maintained Schools by Local Education

Authority Area in England – January 1999) (Provisional)
http://www.dfee.gov.uk/statistics/DB/SBU/b0050/10492e.pdf
(Ethnic Minority Pupils and Pupils for whom English is an
Additional Language 1996/97)
http://www.dfee.gov.uk/statistics/DB/SFR/s0157/sfr20-2000.pdf
(Permanent Exclusions from Schools and Exclusion Appeals,
England 1998/99) (Provisional)
http://www.dfee.gov.uk/statistics/DB/SBU/b0116/pupilabs.pdf
(Statistics Of Education Pupil Absence and Truancy from Schools n
England: 1998/99)
http://www.dfee.gov.uk/statistics/DB/SFR/s0025/sfr-1199.pdf
(Permanent Exclusions from Schools in England 1997/98 and
Exclusion Appeals Lodged by Parents in England 1997/98)
http://www.dfee.gov.uk/statistics/DB/SFR/s0158/sfr21-2000.pdf
(Teacher Sickness Absence in 1999) (Provisional)
http://www.dfee.gov.uk/statistics/DB/SFR/s0022/sfr-0799.pdf
(Teacher Vacancies: Provisional January 1999 statistics)
http://www.dfee.gov.uk/statistics/DB/SFR/s0172/sfr28-2000.pdf
(Participation in Education, Training and Employment by 16–18
Year Olds in England: 1998 and 1999) (29 June 2000)
http://www.dfee.gov.uk/statistics/DB/SBU/b0162/sb02-2000.pdf
(Youth Cohort Study: Education, training and employment of
16–18 year olds in England and the factors associated with non-
participation)
http://www.dfee.gov.uk/statistics/DB/SBU/b0112/educatio.pdf
(Statistics of Education Participation in Education and Training by
Young People Aged 16 and 17 in each Local Area and Region,
England, 1993/94 to 1997/98)
http://www.dfee.gov.uk/statistics/DB/SBU/b0052/youthco.pdf
(Youth Cohort Study: The activities and experiences of 18 year olds:

England and Wales 1998)
http://www.dfee.gov.uk/statistics/DB/SBU/b0051/10581e.pdf
(Youth Cohort Study: The activities and experiences of 16 year olds:
England and Wales 1998)
http://www.dfee.gov.uk/statistics/DB/SBU/b0046/10522e.pdf
(Youth Cohort Study: The activities and experiences of 18 year olds:
England and Wales 1996)

APPENDIX 2
PROFORMA SHEET

Education Services in Deprived and Non-Deprived Areas – Social Exclusion Unit

Literature & Data Review Record Sheet

Title	
Author/s	
Date	
Main Findings	
Aims and Objectives	
Sources of data on educational service/performance (e.g. interviews with head teachers; performance statistics; parents' perceptions, etc.)	
Robustness of methods in relation to the provision of education services (to what extent does method generate valid data on service performance/ provision?)	
What kind of area(s) are considered?	
How are these defined? (to what extent does method generate data on areas and possibility for comparison?)	
Identity and purpose of funder	

Reported implications for policy and practice	
Relevance to national strategy for neighbourhood renewal • *getting people to work* • *getting the place to work (housing, crime, transport, etc.)* • *building a future for young people* • *access to services* • *making Government work better.* *See:* http://www.cabinet-office.gov.uk/seu/1998/bbt/nr1.htm	
Ownership of and access to data	
Potential to address key issues • *evidence of differential or equivalent levels of quality (outputs) and performance (outcomes) in education services in deprived as compared to non-deprived areas* • *the nature of those differences* • *differences in people's access to service* • *the effectiveness, or otherwise, of education services* • *whether effectiveness and access differ in deprived areas for different social groups* • *the causes of differences in delivery and performance and the implications for public policy* • *resource problems faced by public services even when there is no clear link to performance.*	
Most appropriate means of data analysis	
Feasibility and timescale of analysis	